A MARYKNOLL
LITURGICAL YEAR

A MARYKNOLL LITURGICAL YEAR

Reflections on the Readings for Year A

Edited by
Judy Coode and Kathy McNeely

ORBIS BOOKS
Maryknoll, New York 10545

ORBIS BOOKS
Maryknoll, New York 10545

Fathers and Brothers
MARYKNOLL™

Founded in 1970, Orbis Books endeavors to publish works that enlighten the mind, nourish the spirit, and challenge the conscience. The publishing arm of the Maryknoll Fathers and Brothers, Orbis seeks to explore the global dimensions of the Christian faith and mission, to invite dialogue with diverse cultures and religious traditions, and to serve the cause of reconciliation and peace. The books published reflect the views of their authors and do not represent the official position of the Maryknoll Society. To learn more about Maryknoll and Orbis Books, please visit our website at www.maryknollsociety.org.

Copyright © 2013 by Orbis Books

Published by Orbis Books, Box 302, Maryknoll, NY 10545–0302.

Queries regarding rights and permissions should be addressed to:
Orbis Books, P.O. Box 302, Maryknoll, NY 10545–0302.

Manufactured in the United States of America

Library of Congress Cataloging-in-Publication Data
A Maryknoll liturgical year : reflections on the readings for year A /
edited by Judy Coode and Kathy McNeely.
    p.   cm.
Includes index.
ISBN 978-1-62698-032-7
1. Church year meditations. 2. Bible – Meditations. 3. Catholic Church.
Lectionary for Mass (U.S.). Year A. I. Coode, Judy. II. McNeely, Kathy.
BX2170.C55M38 2012
242'.3 – dc23   2012011986

Contents

Preface

As Maryknoll missioners read scripture, their mission experiences—crossing into a new culture, sharing life with new communities—bring fresh meanings of the texts to light. The reflections in the pages that follow describe life in its fullest—sharing the deep pain and struggle that people endure, as well as the hope for "a new heaven and a new earth."

In a world where those who drive the global economy are blind to the grave physical and moral consequences of ignoring earth's natural limits, scores of Maryknoll sisters, priests, brothers, and lay missioners living in resource-poor and indigenous communities have embraced the principle of sufficiency. Reflecting on the words of scripture read from their unique vantage point, Maryknollers describe how people cope with climate changes that have forced them to move, or to give up livelihoods and homeland; they celebrate the solutions people have employed and rejoice in the places where they find hope for the future of the planet.

Maryknollers around the world celebrate diversity as an enriching contribution to inclusive security—even as many in the United States express a desire to exclude those who are different from themselves. Maryknoll missioners around the world celebrate the fact that they are warmly welcomed into the communities in spite of differences in appearance, language, and culture. Missioners often accompany communities struggling with racist practices and tell stories of how looking at "the other" with new and compassionate eyes changed community life for the better. These are the kinds of stories elevated in the reflections included in this book: stories of reconciliation, of interreligious collaboration; stories of ways in which groups have overcome their differences to take on projects that serve the common good.

As it enters into its second century of service to the world, the Maryknoll community celebrates the diversity of gifts offered by other nations and cultures and continues to work shoulder to shoulder with others to build a world where peace and sustainable security is possible. In that new world, immigrant communities feel welcomed and natural resources are not treated as unequally divided spoils that provoke conflict but are used for the common good. It was a privilege to work with the many Maryknoll missioners who contributed these reflections. We hope that in them readers find that the word of God is broken open in new ways.

—*Judy Coode and Kathy McNeely*

First Sunday of Advent

Jeff Hall, former Maryknoll lay missioner

Tanzania

Isaiah 2:1–5; Psalm 122; Romans 13:11–14; Matthew 24:37–44

They shall beat their swords into plowshares, and their spears into pruning hooks; nation shall not lift up sword against nation, neither shall they learn war any more.   —Isaiah 2:4

From 2000 to 2003 I had the privilege to serve as a lay missioner in Tanzania. Like most Maryknollers, I learned incredible lessons about the strength and courage of our brothers and sisters throughout the world who struggle for justice. Those lessons have stuck with me in my work coordinating advocacy and human rights work in Pakistan for a humanitarian aid group. Today, as we begin this Advent season, I'd like to share a bit about one of the countless Pakistanis who rarely make the headlines. As her friend and colleague, I have had the opportunity to watch her incredible work unfold, and to share with her with many of the community mobilization skills I learned during my time as a Maryknoll lay missioner.

A few years ago, on a cool Thursday morning, a humble Pakistani community organizer named Pashmina Haqqani visited the desperately poor village of Kharbooza, in Pakistan's Khyber Pakhtunkhwa province.

Kharbooza borders a particularly volatile tribal area in Pakistan's northwest. It is here in Kharbooza that the forces of moderation subtly confront the forces of extremism. It is here that the forces of pluralism and dialogue confront the forces of oppression and dogma. And it is here that individuals like Pashmina fight the battles that will ultimately determine

Pakistan's fate: battles to save children from premature death, to ensure that every child has a chance at a decent education and that the government responds to the needs of its people. Pashmina knows that if Pakistan can win these battles, the violence that plagues her people will evaporate.

On that Thursday morning, Pashmina went to Kharbooza because she had heard about a desperately poor widow named Hawa whose little boy, Habib, had not been to school in weeks because of a lack of supplies. Poor children like Habib are highly vulnerable to recruitment by extremist militant groups.

As she entered Kharbooza, Pashmina reflected upon the changes she'd seen since she and her team of community mobilizers began working there six months earlier.

She remembered her first day, when the elders of the village flatly refused to allow a women's group to be formed. "We're just getting together for tea," Pashmina insisted. It was a tea party that eventually led sixty women to form an action plan to end corruption in the village school.

She remembered when she began organizing for a village health committee to monitor the quality of services provided to the women in the community. "Our village doesn't need that kind of organization," said the leader of a main political party.

"Well, then I suppose no one will show up for our meetings," answered Pashmina. Since then, the committee has held two public rallies to educate the community on primary health care and improve the quality of the local clinic. Hundreds attended.

Later, she arrived in Kharbooza with a team of civil servants in order to register voters. "Leave," threatened a man invested in the political status quo, "or some harm could come to you."

Pashmina stayed. And to date she and her team have registered more than 25,000 new voters in places that had long been neglected by government. More than 80 percent of those registered are women. Pashmina's team has also helped to repair schools, replant deforested hillsides, and nurture livelihoods for families all across the area.

As Pashmina left Kharbooza that day, she smiled. After meeting with the elders (the very ones who had greeted her so coldly a few months earlier), they decided to contribute to a common fund that would purchase uniforms and supplies for Hawa's son Habib.

As Maryknollers, we meet people like Pashmina all the time—prophetic voices committed to transforming the lives of people who are poor and oppressed. All too often, these brave individuals face dangers we could never imagine. Pashmina was no exception.

Almost four years ago, armed extremists stormed Pashmina's office and brutally murdered seven of her colleagues. As a masked gunman aimed an assault rifle, point blank, at Pashmina's head, he screamed, "Why are you doing this job?"

Pashmina closed her eyes, and recited the most holy words of her faith, which reflect the words of our own First Commandment: "There is no God but God." Miraculously, she was spared.

As we enter this holy season of Advent and prepare for the coming of Jesus, it is worth reflecting on the question put to Pashmina and her brave answer. As with Pashmina, our faith calls on us to do the work of the Lord. Like Pashmina, we have the opportunity to answer courageously. In this Advent season, we, as Christians, have the opportunity to testify that "There is no God but God"—when others worship at the churches of materialism and greed. We say, "There is no God but God" when others lay their offerings before the thrones of violence and hate. And when confronted with the xeno-phobic fear-mongering of those who would pit us, as Chris-tians, against the millions of ordinary Muslims like Pashmina who struggle bravely every day for peace, we can answer con-fidently, "There is no God but God." With these words, we can move one step closer to that day when all will beat their swords into plowshares and their spears into pruning hooks. And the sustainable peace of the kingdom of God will reign.

Feast of the Immaculate Conception (December 8)

Kitty Madden, Maryknoll Affiliate

Nicaragua

Genesis 3:9–15, 20; Psalm 98:1–4; Ephesians 1:3–6, 11–12;
Luke 1:26–38

*He chose us in Christ before the foundation of the world to be
holy and blameless before him in love.*   —*Ephesians 1:4*

It seems to me that these words point up the central theme of
today's liturgy—choose to live through love.

Take a moment to look around the church, to those on your
right and left, those in front of you and those behind you. Yes,
we are the ones about whom this passage speaks. Each and
every one of us has been chosen by our Mother-Father God
from all eternity. Not one has been overlooked. I remember
many times as a young girl hoping against hope that I would
be chosen to make the team for a pick-up game of baseball at
the neighborhood playground. What agony I felt as one after
another was chosen until, finally, I found myself asking God,
"At least don't let me be the last one." However, I know it was
even more painful for my friend Roger, who once struck out
three times in the same inning!

No doubt each one of us has a story about waiting to be
chosen for something. The good news of today's liturgy is that
every single one of us, from all eternity, has definitely been
chosen by God. And for what: for wealth or fame or good for-
tune? Not really. We are told quite simply that each of us has
been chosen to live through love in God's presence.

I invite you today to come and join in spirit with the people
of Nicaragua, in Central America, a people with whom I have

been blessed to live and work these past twenty-five years. They have indeed taught me much about living through love in God's presence.

Here, each year on the eve of the feast of Mary's Immaculate Conception, or in Nicaragua *La Purísima* (the Pure One), people fill the streets of every town and city as they boisterously sing songs in honor of Mary and visit homes where shrines have been lovingly arranged for the novena of days leading up to the feast. Listen to their hymns and to the fire crackers in the background. Note the amazing fireworks that light up the December sky. All this celebration is in honor of the young teenager of Nazareth whose story is told in today's Gospel.

At each Nicaraguan home awaits a family to give out specially made sweets or fruit or a small bowl or handmade gift. The families have made a promise to Mary to do this in return for the answer of some prayer request: health for a loved one who was ill; the return of a son or daughter from the war; a happy death for a parent. . . . It is a bit like the theme of the movie *Pay It Forward*, in which a young boy named Trevor teaches the practice of passing something on to another each time one receives a gift. At each home shrine, people pause their singing to shout out, "*¿Qué causa tanta alegría?*" "What causes so much joy?" And all who hear shout back in one voice, "*La Concepción de María*," "the Conception of Mary." And they end with "*Que viva María; que viva Nicaragua*, "Long live Maria; long live Nicaragua!" How deeply intertwined are the people's love of Mary with their love for their country—a country that in 2012 the U.S. Central Intelligence Agency listed as the second poorest in all of Latin America and where too many families subsist on less than $2 a day.

In today's Gospel, Luke tells us of the visit of the angel, always a symbol that something momentous is about to happen. Mary, as a faithful Jewish woman, is well aware of the Israelite's understanding that they had been chosen to live in accordance with God's covenant. Yes, Mary, too, with all her people, was chosen from all eternity to live in love in God's presence. And in response to the angel's greeting, "Rejoice, you who have been graced," after some initial bewilderment, Mary gives in to what was simply beyond her understanding. "I am the servant of the Lord, let what you have said be done to me."

In this season of Advent, with winter approaching in the northern hemisphere, we are reminded that Mary's story was one of darkness giving birth to light. It was about endless waiting, and about the One who is at the end of all our waiting. God called to Mary:

> I have chosen you.
> Come from the edge of darkness,
> Come from the depth of fear.
> Become the bearer of God.

Will we always understand God's call to us? I think not. But like Mary, we must listen to the longing in our heart. We must listen to what our life tells us it intends to do with us. It is not possible to keep God's grace from coming. But what *is* possible is to miss it, to not look as it brushes past us in our neighborhood or workplace, in the nightly news telling of ways our sisters and brothers in other states or countries have been affected by an earthquake, torrential rains, a mudslide, the collapse of a mine, or the eruption of a volcano. God says to us: Be silent, listen, wait, wonder; something is on the horizon, the likes of which you have never seen. The God-Jesus, who took flesh in Mary, reminds us that to those with eyes and hearts to see, the holy is in our midst, in our lives, and in our very selves.

I invite you today to connect with our sisters and brothers in Nicaragua. As you think of their faith-filled processions through the streets, may you know that, with them and with Mary in her Immaculate Conception, you too have been chosen. You have been chosen to live through love in God's presence. And just imagine the many ways in which this coming week you might pay forward to others this wonderful gift of having being chosen.

Second Sunday of Advent

Br. Martin Shea, MM

Guatemala

Isaiah 11:1–10; Psalm 72:1–2, 7–8, 12–13, 17; Romans 15:4–9;
Matthew 3:1–12

Christ has become a servant . . .   *—Romans 15:8*

In today's reading Paul talks to the Romans and to us about Christ who became a servant, our servant. And in turn we are called to follow him in service to others. Jesus explicitly challenges us: "[Y]ou also should do as I have done to you" (John 13:15).

To respond in service is to meet that challenge in bold faith, but as Ronald Rolheiser says in *The Holy Longing: The Search for a Christian Spirituality*, "I never suspected resurrection to be so painful."

To change is a painful process, or at least sounds painful. But what if the truth is quite the contrary? What if when we touch God in service the fire burns, bring us to life, and heals not just our wounds but all whom God touches through us? It is precisely there in the midst of our hesitancy, fear, confusion, weakness that we catch a glimpse of revelation.

Matthew's Gospel also tells the story of God's servant John the Baptist. He announced the coming of God's beloved servant who would change the entire paradigm of leadership. John embodied the image of the herald described by Isaiah, for he was "[a] voice of one crying out in the wilderness: 'Prepare the way of the Lord, make his paths straight'" (Matthew 3:3). John recognized his role as prophet—not assuming he was the chosen one, but pointing to what was to come: "I baptize you with water for repentance, but one who is more powerful than I is coming after me; I am not worthy to carry his sandals. He will baptize you with the Holy Spirit and fire" (Matthew 3:11).

The Paschal Mystery by nature is painful: if there is no dying, there is no resurrection. We are left with a model of service which is extremely frightening—life threatening in fact. But Jesus teaches his followers that this commitment to service should be embraced and not avoided. Jesus leaves his followers with the gifts of Holy Spirit and fire—a zeal for life that is totally new. As his followers, we are called to be bold, to follow in the same love and service, and know the transforming force and fire that brings life and cauterizes our wounds if we dare to be bold and touch the hem of his garment.

I challenge you to embrace the spirit and fire of Jesus, the call to service, in this season of Advent.

Third Sunday of Advent

Fr. Jim Noonan, MM

Southeast Asia; South Sudan

Isaiah 35:1–6, 10; Psalm 146:6–10; James 5:7–10;
Matthew 11:2–11

Are you the one who is to come, or are we to wait for another?
—*Matthew 11:3*

Today is a special moment in Advent for all of us. John the Baptist—the greatest of all the prophets until then—urges each of us, by his example, to look deeply within our own being to let our gift of prophecy come forth. If this happens it will change what we say and do. It will forever make the world a different place.

Jesus held John in the very highest esteem. He gave John words of praise that he never gave to any other. For Jesus, John was an example for each of us. He is the model that we are to study in order to learn how to be a prophet in our day and in our time.

John's disciples asked Jesus, "Are you the one who is to come, or are we to wait for another?" Jesus' answer is very clear and direct to John and his disciples. He listed all of the signs that had been given from the Old Testament that would accompany the Messiah. These signs were given so that when the Messiah came he would be recognized.

This is an ideal time for us to stop and realize that one of the important reasons why Jesus came was that his light would shine brightly on the social and religious darkness of his day. Jesus was prophet par excellence. That is why he felt such harmony with John the Baptist.

Professor William Barclay defines the prophet as having two main elements: (1) she or he is a person with a message from God, and (2) she or he has the courage to deliver that message. Prophets are people with God's wisdom in their minds, God's truth on their lips, and God's courage in their hearts.

Pope John XXIII was very much in touch with his prophetic mission. He knew that we had entered into a new era of history, so he called the Second Vatican Council. His prayer was that the church in the 1960s could find a new way of being a community of loving service in this new era, to be a church that is at the service of all of God's people, especially those living in poverty. In his encyclical *Mater et Magistra*, he offered a straightforward three-part method for all of us to follow—see, judge, and act—to apply Catholic social teaching to real social concerns, a process often called reading the signs of the times. This is a simple but profound way of discovering the message that God is giving to us and calling us to have the courage to respond.

Reflecting on the signs of the times with a community of faith and love is the best way to discover the message that God gives us to share at this particular moment of history.

During much of my fifty years as a Maryknoll priest I was assigned to Southeast Asia. It was a great joy to have known many laypeople, sisters, brothers, and priests who courageously exercised their prophetic calling. It has made a real difference in our world each time that this prophetic ministry has been exercised in a true and authentic way.

One of my heroes is Fr. Mike Hiegel. We were assigned with many other Maryknollers in a very needy prelature in the southern Philippines. When Maryknoll began to arrive in that area in 1958, the prelature of Tagum, Mindanao, had 500,000 Catholics and no Filipino priests. Father Mike was great for discovering new ways of developing small base Christian communities and involving all the parishioners in a process that would enable each to find a meaningful ministry that the community needed and one that gave each a sense of being a contributor. He understood well what makes a vibrant Christian community. Mike was always challenging all of us to do more and to be more creative so that all would be well served, especially people who were poor.

He accomplished and got others to accomplish so much. His shortcoming, if that is what it should be called, was that he was so busy for others that he had no time to care for himself. He died in his early 50s. We were sad, but Mike was full of joy and peace that he had been gifted with the call to mission.

The most powerful experience of prophecy that came to many of us in the Philippines came from the lay leaders in Tagum. During the dictatorship of Ferdinand Marcos, the parishes in Tagum had become too vibrant for the government. The lay leaders had seen, judged, and acted in very mature ways in responding to the signs of the times as they experienced the oppression of martial law. They were not silent about what they saw and what they saw their neighbors suffering. They knew that there was an evil use of power and corruption at all levels that had to stop. These lay leaders were not involved in partisan politics. They were too busy serving their neighbors during the time of an extremely oppressive governmental administration.

One day out of the blue, sixty of the lay leaders, including several married couples, were arrested. At least 90 percent of the new detainees had children at home. These wonderful Christian leaders were kept in jail for sixty days. All they needed to do to be released was to testify that their parish priests were working for a new type of government structure.

The military leaders of the area would come at night after the court hearings to try to make deals with a selected few of the lay leaders, but their efforts were fruitless.

The hearings went on because the officials felt that someone would eventually break and give false testimony. This did not happen. One of the pastors, so very sad to see these fine people suffer such injustice, told a small group, "Tell them what they want to hear; we understand," but the lay leaders responded immediately, "We have our integrity."

Finally the authorities realized that the leaders would stay as long as it took for them to understand with whom they were dealing: These were followers of the tradition of John the Baptist and Jesus who had come to serve others so that all might have life.

It all ended as quickly as it began. After two months of failing to get someone to give false testimony, the authorities simply released the leaders. The sixty leaders left the detainment center in Davao City full of love and fire. They went home more committed to serve their communities than when they were arrested.

Let us pray on this third Sunday of Advent that we will open our hearts wide as we begin this new liturgical year. We ask this Christmas that we will be prepared, as never before, to welcome Jesus into that deepest depth of our being so that the light that Jesus brings will let us more fully appreciate that our world will only become full of peace and loving service if that begins in the hearts of each of us. What a different world we will have when finally we have learned to follow Jesus who is our way, our truth, our life.

Fourth Sunday of Advent

Judy Coode

Maryknoll Office for Global Concerns

Isaiah 7:10–14; Psalm 24:1–6; Romans 1:1–7; Matthew 1:18–24

O house of David! Is it too little for you to weary mortals, that you weary my God also? . . . The Lord himself will give you a sign. Look, the young woman is with child and shall bear a son, and shall name him Immanuel.
                                  —*Isaiah 7:13–14 and Matthew 1:23*

Today's readings present the Big Reveal: God will prove God's love and fidelity for all creation by the fantastic miracle of a virgin birth. The fact that a dozen other virgin birth stories exist in other faith traditions does nothing to diminish the significance of this promise; nor does it negate the wonder of the Incarnation that occurred in Palestine two thousand years ago. There's a comfort that humans have such similar responses in our need to understand our connection to our Creator.

Growing up as an obedient Jew, Joseph must have known about Isaiah's prophecy, so when he is told in a dream that he is to have an integral role in pulling this whole thing together, he must have been, at the very least, surprised, and most likely petrified. Joseph, in his obedience to God's will, had to do some quick comprehension work: This baby would not be the warrior, David-like king they were expecting to save them from Rome's oppression. God had something different in mind this time, something much bigger. Joseph was not going to have exactly the sort of life he was expecting; he had just agreed to protect and provide for . . . God.

Also, despite being faithful to the law, according to the Gospel, Joseph circumvented the rules and accepted Mary as his wife—he took God's path rather than the path established by the powers that be. This was a necessary and humane breach, much like the "offenses" committed by volunteers along the U.S.–Mexico border who leave water for migrants or who provide rides to health clinics for ill migrants. These folks, often connected to faith-based programs, are practicing Christianity at its most basic, and sadly they are oftentimes arrested for it.

Every year thousands of people travel up through Central America and then through Mexico, making their way into the United States, where they hope to find employment or opportunity or, sometimes, to reunite with a parent or loved one. Maryknoll sisters who work at a clinic in Guatemala see migrants on a regular basis, including women who confess their expectation of sexual attack during their trek north. This is a heartbreakingly accurate expectation. A Maryknoll lay missioner who lived and worked in Mexico near the border with Texas tells of overhearing a weeping teenage boy, who didn't look older than fifteen, on the phone with his mother. He was begging her to let him come home and not make the attempt to cross (which either would send him through an unforgiving desert or possibly across the Rio Grande). The mother insisted the boy needed to continue—he was the best chance the family had to earn some money.

"In the past ten years, thousands of migrants have died along the Mexico–U.S. border. Draconian immigration policies, instituted in the mid-1990s, sealed major urban crossing areas in the southern United States, and forced migrants into deadly desert regions. Policy makers assumed that the desert would prove a deterrent to undocumented migration, but tragically, that has not been the case" (Maryknoll leadership statement on migration, 2006).

According to the Climate Justice and Migration Working Group of the Mobilization for Climate Justice, "Governmental policies and corporate practices impact communities around the world, especially those most vulnerable. . . . National responses to the increasing phenomena of global migration . . . prioritize national security concerns and immigration restrictions, including for those who are forced to migrate."

What is our role as Christians in caring for these siblings of ours? What does the "law" tell us to do? What do we hear when we hear God's voice? God continues to offer a Big Reveal: God is found on the faces of those who cross borders, who walk this earth with us, and who suffer mightily for a life of dignity. Will we have the compassion and the vulnerability to accept this and respond?

Christmas Mass at Midnight

Cecilia Espinoza, Maryknoll lay missioner

Chile; United States

Isaiah 9:1–6; Psalm 96:1–3, 11–13; Titus 2:11–14; Luke 2:1–14

To you is born this day in the city of David a Savior, who is the Messiah, the Lord. This will be a sign for you: you will find a child wrapped in bands of cloth and lying in a manger."
                                                                    —Luke 2:11–13

Christmas is a time of traditions, a time of joy, a time to remember how we are cherished by an all-loving God who offers salvation to all, and that peace is possible. Christmas is about Jesus, the greatest sign of God's love for the human family and all creation. It probably sounds a bit obvious, but in today's world we tend to confuse the spirit of Christmas with the unfortunate draw of consumerism and the message to buy and give expensive gifts, often more than we can afford.

As we celebrate the gift of Christmas, I recall a story that happened in April 1999. I was then working as a family therapist in a holistic center for adolescents in the diocese of Linares, a rural and poor area in the south of Chile. Created by the diocese to receive adolescents from the area who suffered tremendous difficulties—parents disappeared, tortured, or imprisoned during the seventeen-year military dictatorship of Augusto Pinochet—the center was the response of the local church and several volunteer medical professionals to the lack of places where the needs of these young people could be met. As the years went by, the center broadened its scope of attention to all youth of the poor and marginalized areas of the rural city of Linares in order for them to receive the proper mental and physical care.

One day I was doing the intake of a sixteen-year-old boy whose name for this story will be Mario, who had manifested several behavioral problems in school since early December 1998. He lost his father in a very tragic work accident and was not able to cope with what this sudden loss meant to him and to the rest of the family. This young man, his mother, and siblings started a process of family therapy to integrate this awful reality into their lives and hopefully accept the fact that the father was no longer with them and all that this signified in their lives. We had many sessions together with the entire family as well as with individuals.

For the mother, whose name for this story is Rosa, the two main questions were "Why if I have been a devoted wife and mother, has this happened to me?" And "Why if I have been a committed and faithful Christian, has God permitted this?" During this time, I invited Rosa to participate in a weekly women's support group, which she did, little by little sharing her pain, anger, and sadness. She never missed a session, and she was not only supported but also gave support to others who needed it.

In late November 1999, she did not show up, which raised questions for the whole group. We feared something had occurred. I went to her house, but no one was there, which concerned me even more. Just before the next session, Rosa's brother came to the center and told me that Mario's older brother, Jose, had died of a late-diagnosed leukemia. Members of the support group and I went to accompany Rosa at the funeral; as we arrived, one of her brothers was carrying her in his arms. She was not capable of walking.

As time went on and after several visits, I invited her to continue participating in the support group. She said she needed some time and that she would return when she was ready. Shortly after Christmas, she returned to the group and told what had happened. Her son was hospitalized when he became severely ill. In the hospital she did not leave his side. She and the family were informed that he had only a few days to live. She shared with the group that her son's illness and impending death made her realize what a tremendous gift life is.

After the death of her husband and now the death of her son, her profound faith helped her to realize what a gift loved ones are and that one must live thinking each day of the precious gift that life is. We need to enjoy it, appreciate it, love it, and give thanks to God each day while we have it. Rosa said, "I made the decision to resolve any issues I had with my son and talk to him, ask for forgiveness and forgive. I told him how much I loved him and promised never to leave him alone. I promised that I would always be with him in thought and spirit." Tears filled her eyes as she expressed how much she missed him but said that she felt peace in her heart and the strong presence of God accompanying her.

There is no doubt that for Rosa and her family Christmas will always stir mixed emotions and be remembered with longing and sadness. They will always feel the painful absence of two dear family members, but will also experience tremendous gratitude for the gift of life—and having each other to love.

Jesus is the one who rescued this family, and Rosa clearly understood this. The angel said to the shepherds: "I am bringing you good news of great joy for all the people: to you is born this day in the city of David a Savior, who is the Messiah, the Lord." There is no doubt that Jesus' joy is that of the Resurrection. There is no doubt that it was the risen Christ born in Bethlehem who accompanied this family. Our heavenly joy is that which we feel after having undergone the trials of the cross—with Christ. Jesus is the Savior and bearer of peace. The peace that Jesus brought is not just the removal of conflict; the peace that Jesus brings is that which helps us to face and solve the conflict. It is the opportunity to encounter the other and look for the common good. Jesus is the liberator of all human conditions and the highest hope of eternal life for all.

This is the fundamental message of Christmas that brings hope and joy: we are not alone in our loneliness and our search for unity, integration, solidarity, and reconciliation of all and with all. God-with-us, Emmanuel, is here: "to you is born this day in the city of David a savior, who is the Messiah, the Lord."

The message of Jesus came to me and to the women's group in the very sad yet profound story of a poor but faith-filled woman from the marginalized areas of Linares, Chile. She had lost so much, had next to nothing of materials goods, yet processed the profound understanding of the message of Jesus, the message of what Christmas is all about.

Feast of the Holy Family

Fr. Leo Shea, MM

Jamaica

Sirach 3:2–6, 12–14; Psalm 128:1–5; Colossians 3:12–21; Matthew 2:13–15, 19–23

As God's chosen ones, holy and beloved, clothe yourselves with compassion, kindness, humility, meekness, and patience.
—*Colossians 3:12*

One of Matthew's earliest story of Jesus, Mary, and Joseph begins with an urgency to flee. Suddenly the Holy Family is a displaced family. They are a family on the run, like so many families and children in our world. Through God's grace and intervention, the hand of God was upon them: "remain there until I tell you" (Matthew 2:13). Then they safely returned to their home in Nazareth, where Jesus' childhood took place a secure, and caring environment.

In Jamaica, West Indies, and other areas of the Caribbean, displaced and abandoned children are a large part of our reality. There is a Caribbean saying, "Any man can be your father, but you have only one mother." On the island, 90 percent of all children are born out of wedlock. When a child is disabled, it is not uncommon for the child to be abandoned. The churches and compassionate people feel the urgency to respond out of love to protect these children from further harm.

I am chaplain at Blessed Assurance Orphanage for special children, located in western Jamaica. The rural orphanage is one of thirteen homes in Jamaica operated by a Catholic institution called Mustard Seed Communities. Many children in the home cannot walk, talk, or feed themselves. The caregivers are women of different denominations. Each month we celebrate through praise and worship our common faith and love for God and these children. We celebrate our gifts of diversity, our gifts of faith, hope, and love trying to imitate the Holy Family. Blessed Assurance is sacred space for all.

These Jamaican women express their natural gifts by washing, feeding, clothing, and, most of all, by loving these special children. One can see the transformation of a child after several weeks in the orphanage.

Some time ago an eleven-year-old girl was left at our home, her tiny body limp and covered from head to toe with scabs. The child was blind and HIV positive and she could not hear very well. So our caregivers bathed her, fed her, and put her to bed with clean sheets. She also received badly needed medical care. In the beginning, she cried day and night. After a few weeks, she sat up and began to feed herself. After a few months, her scabs were gone, and she began to smile and laugh. If you were a first-time visitor here, you would think that this little girl is perfectly healthy. She is just one of the miracles that transform life at Blessed Assurance.

When tourists leave their cruise ships for a visit to the island of Jamaica, they are often shuttled away to discount stores inside our gated malls. That's so they can search for the perfect gift at the perfect price in safety. Of course, visitors usually find what they're looking for—except for Jamaica's most precious gifts, our caregivers and special children.

Blessed Assurance also is a gated community where the children are secure, watched over, and loved. The ecumenical team of caregivers brings their gifts of faith and compassion to their daily tasks. These women act as parents for these handicapped children. The diversity of gifts, which also includes their spiritual songs and spontaneous prayers, makes for a much enriched community.

I am delighted to see that the small Catholic Church in Jamaica, which is working with other faiths, can play such a big role in providing community services. Blessed Assurance is one of many Christian institutions for the sick and needy across the island. So much is achieved because so many gifts of compassion are shared by people of faith.

Matthew reminds us in today's Gospel that after Joseph's second dream, the Holy Family went to a town called Nazareth, where Jesus' childhood was safe from harm. Today Mustard Seed Communities, such as Blessed Assurance, are places where Jamaican children are safe from harm, secure and cared for. In the caregivers' dreams, these little ones are to be loved as God's children. Our orphanage of Blessed Assurance is a real family of self-sacrificing staff and blessed children. These beautiful children are not only constantly watched over by God, but also these vulnerable children are loved by dedicated caregivers who serve as their mothers, not unlike the child in today's Gospel story of the Holy Family.

They say that no exercise is better for the human heart than reaching down to lift up another person. I have certainly learned that lesson over the years in Jamaica from committed sisters of various faiths with the same common spirit of compassion.

Feast of Mary, Mother of God (January 1)

Sr. Teresa Alexander, MM

Central America

Numbers 6:22–27; Psalm 67:2–3, 5–6, Galatians 4:4–7;
Luke 2:16–21

*The shepherds returned, glorifying and praising God for all they
had heard and seen, as it had been told them.* —Luke 2:20

Our Maryknoll Sisters' motto is "Making God's love visible."
On this beautiful feast of Mary, Mother of God, Mary is the
first to make God's love visible. How? Her quick trip to her
cousin Elizabeth to greet her and to stay and help.

I was assigned to my first mission in Panama in 1959. I went
with the idea of teaching. Of course, I knew everything—or
thought I did! The first lesson I learned was hospitality. The
people living in poverty were so generous to me. My first trip
to one of the pueblos was about an hour and a half away by
horse. Anna sent her son to pick me up. I rode on the horse
with the little ten-year-old. It was a day's journey.

I was taken to visit all the Catholic families in the pueblo.
Each family offered me a drink and something to eat. Everywhere I went I accepted. I had never been fed so well! When we
arrived back at Anna's house late in the afternoon she offered
me a huge plate of chicken and rice. I thought to myself surely
she will understand that I just could not eat any more, so I
refused her plate. But she was quick to tell me that if I did not
accept her dinner I was rejecting her! So I took it and ate as
much as I could. I spent the night in her humble home on a
bed she made with bamboo and a little mat.

Later, as I continued visiting the homes in the different villages and accepting their rice and beans, yucca or plantain, I

realized that I did not have to eat everything on every plate. One night, someone in the family who had been watching picked up my half-finished plate and shared what was left over with other family members. I learned that they were so generous that they had given me their meal.

As Mary went out to her cousin so we as missioners, all of us, must go out to share and receive. Paul's letter to the Galatians tells us, "God has sent the Spirit of his Son into our hearts" (Galatians 4–6). Yes, Jesus is always present in all of our hearts, no matter where we live, here or in other countries. We must be the hands, feet, and voice carrying God's love to all. Mary certainly carried God's love to her cousin and received a beautiful blessing from Elizabeth. We have received countless blessings from others in our lives. In our Gospel reading today we hear, The shepherds "went with haste and found Mary and Joseph, and the child lying in the manger. When they saw this, they made known what had been told them about this child" (Luke 2:16–17). They went, they saw, they heard the good news, and they shared it with others.

We have many people in our world who have not heard this good news—people who have not heard and others who have heard and do not understand. There are people suffering and sick; those who make very little salary for their hard work, those who lack education and recreation, those who earn barely enough in one day just to feed their family that evening, those who have no money for medicine. Is this justice? Is this love? Some may live close to us: others live farther away. How about the immigrants who come to our country?

There are many ways we can share our love and our faith with others. Maybe one of the best ways is through acts of kindness. People will find the best ways to solve their difficulties as soon as they realize their human dignity. It is possible to change our own lives and to have an influence on the lives of others. Love grows, love blossoms as soon as it is given. All of us can make love visible, help spread it, and make love blossom. There will be struggles, pain, and death. It will not be as easy as it might sound. Did not Jesus suffer and die for our freedom?

Just as fire brings warmth and light, we are in mission to bring love and light. We share our faith, our light, and our love, not to preach or impose our customs but to share by actions so others can take hold of it and carry forward the faith, truth, love, and embrace until it fills the whole world. "The shepherds returned, glorifying and praising God for all they had heard and seen, as it had been told them" (Luke 2:20).

Feast of the Epiphany

Fr. Jack Sullivan, MM

Hong Kong

Isaiah 60:1–6; Psalm 72:1–2, 7–8, 10–13; Ephesians 3:2–3, 5–6;
Matthew 2:1–12.

*When they saw that the star had stopped, they were overwhelmed
with joy. On entering the house, they saw the child with Mary
his mother. . . . They offered him gifts of gold, frankincense, and
myrrh.*   *—Matthew 2:10–11*

Today we celebrate the Epiphany of Jesus—the appearance,
manifestation, and revelation of God among us in Christ Jesus.
For many of our sisters and brothers in the Eastern Christian
churches, this Feast of the Manifestation of Jesus to the Magi
from the East is the primary celebration of God revealed in
flesh and blood to all the peoples of the earth.

This Epiphany story, like any good story, like the parables
to be composed by the child of Mary when he became an
adult, carries a meaning put to words, a message heard and
understood according to the capacity, culture, and creativity of
its hearers. "Magi," "gifts of gold, frankincense and myrrh,"
"star," the seeing of "the child with Mary his mother"— all
are ingredients of the story that have been used to convey
meanings still unfolding in the awareness of those who believe
that the Epiphany is still taking place. The joyous message of
God among and within us remains the same; we the hearers
change as our awareness of life around us continues to emerge.

Who could the "Magi" be now? These non-Jews, non-
believers in the Gospel story could be the theorists within and

outside our faith traditions who are helping us see creation as infinitely large and small, infinitely complex and always emerging, all at the same time.

Gold, frankincense and myrrh, as gifts of this earth, were and are precious in our eyes as minerals and plants. These gifts announce that the ever-creating and loving God, revealed among us in Jesus, is among us in all of our sisters and brothers, in every creature of the earth, in the earth itself.

The "star" tells us, who are now aware that our star, the sun, is but one of billions of stars in our galaxy that in turn is but one of billions of galaxies, that God is revealed in all of creation. We are being "star-tled" with a growing awareness that our universe seems to be ever expanding. Our brother Augustine's words of the fourth century are now the words of mystics and scientists: "God is an infinite circle whose center is everywhere and whose circumference is nowhere."

Seeing the child with Mary his mother is an invitation for us to see. This feast of the Epiphany reminds us that we, like the Magi, are challenged to see the child with Mary his mother, in every human being of every race, culture, and religion, in the old and young, in female and male, in gay and straight, in friend and enemy, in family and stranger. The child Jesus reminds us that God is revealed in every person, and that relating to even the "least" of these is relating to God incarnate among us.

We are invited and challenged to see the child in every creature of the earth, in the air we breathe, the water in and around us, and earth itself, which sustains our lives. With Francis of Assisi we respect and honor God incarnate and revealed in these so often abused sisters and brothers. We are challenged to live in harmony with, and without domination of, all creatures of the earth. We are becoming aware that although we need the earth and its gifts for our survival, the earth can easily do without us!

God is always revealed to us; God revealed in Christ Jesus calls us to be aware of this ever-revealing God. We discover God and name the discovery revelation. Scripture, history, experience seem to be telling us that God always and every-where reveals self in and through whatever is available at a particular time and in the words, culture, and people of that time. There is nothing, no experience, no joy or catastrophe, no happiness or suffering, no destructive behavior or loving sacrifice, no life or death that is "outside" of God who is in and within all, not as the all-powerful one but as the all-com-passionate One, ever creating and taking flesh in and through every creature.

God is never limited or constricted by our understanding, teachings, and religions. The Magi knew this, Mary knew this, the earth and the cosmos already know it; we are still learning; we are still growing in awareness. Our gifts of gold, frankin-cense, and myrrh symbolize our response to this awareness. We respond in hope by our respectful relationships with all human beings, all creatures of the earth, the earth and the cosmos. We respond in hope and compassion. We are Magi, giving the gifts of our lives, seeing with Mary the ongoing Epiphany of God among us.

Baptism of the Lord

Kathy McNeely, former Maryknoll lay missioner

Guatemala; Maryknoll Office for Global Concerns

Isaiah 42:1–4, 6–7; Psalm 29:1–4, 9–10; Acts 10:34–38; Matthew 3:13–17

And a voice from heaven said, "This is my Son, the Beloved, with whom I am well pleased." —*Matthew 3:17*

Today's readings highlight Jesus as the servant leader—called for the victory of justice, formed by God as a "light to the nations"—one who is sent "to open the eyes that are blind, to bring out the prisoners from the dungeon, from the prison those who sit in darkness." Jesus models for us the role of a leader as one who humbly serves those in need. Living in Washington, D.C., I cannot help but think of all the ways in which the world would be a better place if only our leaders in political, social, and economic spheres would embrace Jesus' servant-leader model.

We have too many examples today of how world leaders have used circumstances, people, and even the planet all for their own benefit and personal gain. Politically, some newly elected congressional leaders have in effect stated that their goal is not to serve the public by legislating but to serve party politics by obstructing legislative processes. At the same time a handful of people with tremendous economic wealth push for continuous growth that ignores earth's limits and its need to rest and regenerate. Ecologically, people, cultures, and species are lost, land is destroyed, and waterways are polluted in search of economic growth and the energy sources to drive our frenetic society.

In spite of the human, economic, and ecological suffering, we are bombarded by constant messages driving us to grow more and get bigger without questioning the model's viability. As long as those in power benefit from the system there is little incentive to change, and it is easy for those in power to ignore the torment suffered by the majority and the planet.

Jesus' model of leadership is decidedly different. Everything about Jesus' life invites his followers into a new way of seeing. He turns expectations of a messiah totally upside down when he is born to a mother forced to give birth in a stable after being turned away from other lodging possibilities. He is a humble tradesman who grows up in Nazareth. He reaches out to untouchable people including those who are outsiders, sick, lame, and mentally ill, and he changes their lives forever. He wanders around the territory with a group of laborers and other followers who would not cut the mustard in the theological, philosophical, and political debates of their time, yet he teaches them new interpretations of ancient scriptures.

In the encounter with John the Baptist described in today's Gospel, John recognized Jesus as the leader for whom he waited, the one without sin who was chosen by God, but Jesus humbly insists on being baptized by John, and, in doing so, to completely submit to God's plan of salvation for all. From here Jesus goes out into the desert. On a forty-day fast he reconnects with the beauty of all God's creation and with his mission. Though his human form is tested and tempted, he remains true to his mission as servant leader, modeling a totally new kind of leadership for the world, one filled with true compassion while demonstrating a unique kind of strength found in weakness.

We are at a moment in history when a new way of seeing is desperately needed to move us all from exploitation, greed, and pride toward right relationships for individuals and all of creation, toward shifting the focus from material goods to holistic well-being, from excess to sufficiency, from competition to cooperation, from pursuing privilege to serving the common good, and toward reverence for all life. Just as Jesus shifted the meaning of kingship with a new model of leadership, we desperately long for a shift of priorities to identify what is truly important.

In 2009, the Faith Economy Ecology Transformation Working Group wrote a statement to spell out this new vision and the steps needed to get there. Since then, over eighty religious groups, congregations, and organizations have joined them in endorsing a vision of a "closed-loop" economic system that fits within earth's ecological limits and more authentically serves human needs. This shift in thinking is long overdue and points to a new kind of leadership—more akin to that which Jesus modeled—that is urgently needed.

The prophet Isaiah looked forward to a new messiah intimately connected with God: "I am the Lord, I have called you in righteousness, I have taken you by the hand and kept you; I have given you as a covenant to the people, a light to the nations, to open the eyes that are blind, to bring out the prisoners from the dungeon, from the prison those who sit in darkness" (Isaiah 42:6–7).

It does indeed feel like a dark time, but we know that God is with us and is constantly making all things new. Please join me today in praying that the leaders of our world may embrace new models of leading us into the light.

Second Sunday in Ordinary Time

Sr. Cathy Encarnacion, MM

Philippines

Isaiah 49:3, 5–6; Psalm 40:2, 4, 7–10; First Corinthians 1:1–3; John 1:29–34

He drew me up from the desolate pit, out of the miry bog, and set my feet upon a rock, making my steps secure.   —Psalm 40:2

The readings today collectively emphasize the fundamental need for community in our relationships with one another and with God. As a returning missioner to my country of origin, the Philippines, and now working as the director of the Maryknoll Ecological Center in Baguio, I know that the effects of recent typhoons highlight this need.

On September 30, 2009, a tropical storm named Pepeng entered Philippine territory just days after typhoon Ondoy caused havoc in the capital, Manila, and in some two dozen other provinces. Pepeng, however, escalated in strength as it joined other tropical storms in Asia to become a super typhoon, leaving in its wake 492 people killed, 54,000 houses destroyed, some 372,695 families displaced, and over $620 million in damages to agriculture, public works, and private property, mostly in the northern part of Luzon.

In October 2010, another super typhoon, Megi, hit the country, specifically the northern part, again damaging rice crops and structures and cutting power lines for days. It was notable that fewer lives were lost as typhoon warnings were issued much earlier, endangered communities were evacuated in time, and several companies closed early to allow employees to go home to their families to secure their dwellings.

The strong storms keep happening: Tropical storm Washi killed nearly 1,300 people in December 2011, and over 1,000 people were killed by typhoon Bopha in December 2012, with damages estimated to cost over $588 million.

The statistics present a very stark image, and yet that image pales in comparison to that of several dozen families making efforts to live harmoniously together in evacuation centers with areas suited for half their number. Starker still is the image of those who have attended wake after wake in communities where whole families of three to eight members were all buried alive by landslides as they slept in their homes the night of the storm.

At times, I cannot help but feel upset, resigned, or even hopeless when I see the effects of the ecological backlash that hurt and destroy the lives of the people least guilty of the environmental destruction that contributed to cause the damage. In the Cordilleras, the area most affected by typhoon Pepeng, it is common knowledge that open-pit mining by transnational companies, indiscriminate and excessive logging by concessionaires, land conversions from forest to residential areas, and unabated use of insecticides and pesticides are the primary reasons for many environmental problems. Yet, none of the mentioned activities are thus far restricted in any significant way by the government. Greatest profit at the least cost is still the slogan.

Happily, as Isaiah in our first reading today proclaims, it is through the suffering people of Israel that God's glory shines, I am constantly awed by the resilience of the most downtrodden people who live in poverty. An obvious example for me was when we were trying to assess the extent of damages and visited communities to help comfort grieving families and direct donations to evacuation centers in areas afflicted by

Pepeng. My attention was caught by our staff members who quietly gathered cans of goods and pounds of rice they had on their own shelves to donate to a sister of another staff member who had to be evacuated as the foundation of her small house was split in two.

After Pepeng, all of us at the center went in twos and threes to visit one another's homes and communities to see if there were ways we could help better secure the houses. Those of us on staff decided to improve our varying levels of ecological knowledge through actual case work. We found that some places needed to have better riprapping, others more vegetation with good root systems to prevent erosion, and others needed similar ecological repairs. And as we were making these evaluations, some of their neighbors were drawn to the task and started asking the staff how to improve their own areas. Thus, we found ourselves reaching out to others doing God's will, and we sang a new song that God put in our mouths, to use the psalmist's words today. Although we were crying ourselves, we did not restrain our lips, for God was with us, allowing us to open our ears and proclaim justice—to promote right relationships among all that lives.

Although working with the land to find healthier practices through biodynamic farming and investing great efforts to help indigenous peoples in Baguio reclaim their cultural identities and heritage are not the easiest tasks, nor popular choices in the ever-growing cosmopolitan trend of our world, we feel this is how we say, "Here we are Lord; we come to do your will." Like Paul in his letter to the people of Corinth, we claim no authority from anywhere or anyone else than Jesus Christ, the Prince of Peace, that as Christians we strive to follow his path of holiness, to be about peace, as we believe that true peace can only come from justice.

In today's Gospel John emphasizes the indwelling of the Spirit in Jesus, a clear image of the intimacy of God and Jesus. We, like John, are called to keep witnessing to this truth, the greatest act of love: God incarnated. For although we will never come to know or understand this mystery to any great lengths, we can make known this great love in how we live our lives, in how we do justice, love kindness, and walk humbly with our God.

Third Sunday in Ordinary Time

Susan Gunn

Maryknoll Office for Global Concerns

Isaiah 8:23–9:3; Psalm 27:1, 4, 13–14; First Corinthians 1:10–13, 17; Matthew 4:12–23

The people who sat in darkness have seen a great light, and for those who sat in the region and shadow of death light has dawned.   —*Matthew 4:16*

The Gospel of Matthew today tells us that Jesus is the fulfillment of the prophet Isaiah's words: "'The people who sat in darkness have seen a great light, and for those who sat in the region and shadow of death light has dawned.' From that time Jesus began to proclaim, 'Repent, for the kingdom of heaven has come near.'" Later in the Gospel reading Jesus says "Follow me" to Peter and Andrew, and then James and John. They immediately left their nets and followed Jesus. Immediately they turned away from their livelihood and followed the light. After that, Jesus went throughout Galilee, a chaotic place, teaching and healing every disease and sickness. The light of Christ shone brightly amid the darkness of that community.

Where is the light today? Peter Maurin, who cofounded the Catholic Worker movement, wrote that he went out to the streets of New York to mingle with the workers and unemployed, hoping to share God's love with them, to practice what Maurin called, "the art of human contact." We often interact with each other without making any real contact. Maurin was talking about the interpersonal contact that flows from, and leads to, a recognition of the deepest, innermost "I" that resides in the heart of every person. Such contact nourishes our humanity. We need it. It is a deliberate act. This is what the Apostles experienced with Jesus in Galilee, to compel them to leave everything and start a new life with Jesus.

How do we come out of the darkness? If our communities do not recognize and value all members, the light that is within each of us is scattered in the darkness. If I do not make real human contact with the members of my community, do I miss Jesus when he calls me to come follow him? If I do not act justly, show mercy, and love tenderly will there be justice, mercy, and love for me, for anyone? Jean Vanier, the founder of L'Arche, an international federation of group homes for people with developmental disabilities and those who assist them, wrote "We are not called by God to do extraordinary things, but to do ordinary things with extraordinary love."

Extraordinary love is the way out of the darkness. Maryknoll missionaries do not gain fame for doing extraordinary things, but rather they are known for their extraordinary love. During my years in mainland China as a volunteer sponsored by the National Council of Churches, my work was to train middle school teachers of English who were studying at poor, rural teacher training colleges in counties long closed to contact with the outside world. These teachers had never met a native speaker of English and had marginal mastery of the subject they were supposed to teach. Most of them were depressed about the prospect of a life spent teaching middle school in poor rural communities. I was asked many times why I, a privileged person from the United States, came to live and work there. I learned that the best answer was, "To be with you." This answer was the first step in opening the door for me to join the community, to be the light, to call forth light out of the darkness, within me and within each other.

The light of Christ is why, despite the darkness around us, we are a people of hope. May we see the light that is radiating around us and join with the light, as a people forgiven, restored, and renewed!

Feast of the Presentation of the Lord

Chad Ribordy, former Maryknoll lay missioner

Brazil

Malachi 3:1–4; Psalm 24:7–10; Hebrews 2:14–18;
Luke 2:22–40 or 2:22–32

*And they offered a sacrifice according to what is stated in the
law of the Lord, "a pair of turtledoves or two young pigeons."*
—Luke 2: 24

One of my least favorite Christmas songs when I was a kid was
"The Twelve Days of Christmas." First of all, I was angry that
we never really got twelve more days of gift-giving like the
song seemed to promise. Secondly, I couldn't really understand why anyone would want presents like maids a-milking
or lords a-leaping. And what were turtledoves anyway? Today,
nearly a month since the twelve days of Christmas have passed,
here are these birds again in the Gospel reading from Luke.
What could possibly be so significant about this animal? A
quick search through biblical commentaries reveals that the
turtledove was the poor person's offering to God. The rich
person's offering was a lamb or a kid—the goat kind, not
human!

Gifts of the poor. I wonder how the priests of the Temple
received such offerings. I rather imagine it was like the way
I opened up the Christmas present from my grandmother.
Every year it was the same thing: socks and underwear. Yes,
essentials, I never got those things from anyone else, and had
it not been for my grandmother, I would have been pretty
uncomfortable down under. But still, not that exciting. I knew
my grandmother did not have a lot of money, and it was her

way of expressing love for me, but I would have much rather had a Hotwheels car. So, turtledoves, that's nice, but bring on the lamb!

Gifts of the poor—does anyone really want them? I never really thought about that question until I lived and worked as a Maryknoll lay missioner among those on the margins of society in the city of Sao Paulo, Brazil. I wore many hats during my thirteen years in Brazil, one of them being a member of the Pastoral da Crianca team, a ministry of the Catholic Church to families with few resources. Most of the team members have few resources themselves. Every month the team would gather for a meeting to discuss the difficulties we saw in the community after visits to the families. Interestingly, our team leader Catarina would begin each session with the litany of tasks she had to do, and how she was just feeling so overwhelmed because she could not keep up with everything, including her responsibilities as team leader. This would go on for some ten to fifteen minutes, and I would always think to myself, "Well let's get this meeting going so you will have more time to do your other things." And then someone else would chime in about all of their difficulties and we would spend another 15 minutes with that. This little ritual drove me crazy! I didn't really get what was going on until a conversation I had with one of the team members whose name was Ze (a nickname for Joseph, a main character in today's reading).

One day I asked Ze why he volunteered for this ministry. His response was this: "I know there are people with money in this world, and are able to give lots of nice gifts. Sometimes they bring food and clothes to our community. I don't have those kinds of resources, but I still want to give back to my community. The one thing that I do have is time. My time is my gift to this community." I reflected on that, especially in light of the meetings. What appeared to me as being a supreme waste of time was really perhaps a way for Catarina and the others to express the preciousness of their gift, the gift of time.

Gifts of the poor. Did I value that gift? Or was the meeting's agenda more important?

Today's Feast of the Presentation celebrates Joseph and Mary offering the gift of their son to the Jewish community. A poor boy, a poor gift—did anyone notice? Did anyone care? Probably not many that day. Perhaps they were too busy making their own offerings at the Temple, following their own agendas, not noticing the gift being unveiled before them. But two people caught it: Simeon and Anna, both older persons whose pace of life perhaps allowed them to catch the subtleties and mysteries of life unfolding around them.

We all have gifts, and every time we gather as a faith community we celebrate the great diversity of the gifts around us. Yet it often seems that in this world of ours, some gifts are celebrated more than others.

Turtledoves, socks, underwear, time, labor in the fields, factories, and streets: Does anyone want them? Who could live without them?

Does anyone value such gifts? What would this world look like if we did?

Fifth Sunday in Ordinary Time

P. Thomas McGuire, Maryknoll Affiliate

Chicago

Isaiah 58:7–10; Psalm 112:4–9, First Corinthians 2:1–5;
Matthew 5:13–16

*If you offer your food to the hungry and satisfy the needs of the
afflicted, then your light shall rise in the darkness and your
gloom be like the noonday."*   —Isaiah 58:10

Several years ago as pastoral minister in St. Benedict Parish,
Highland Park, Michigan, I had a personally transformative
conversation with an African American woman. She lived on
a street with many burned-out houses, in a neighborhood
known for crime and lacking in beauty. My feeling as I walked
toward her home was one of desolation and gloom; I certainly did not see any shining light in the darkness of that
neighborhood.

Our conversation lasted only a few minutes, but it made a
lasting impression. We talked about the mystery of God and
how blessed she was despite her health problems caused by
the unhealthy conditions in the factory where she worked and
the deteriorating neighborhood where she lived and raised her
family. She spoke of the good people around her working to
make things better in the neighborhood. Her joy-filled attitude showed none of the desolation and gloom I felt. She was
a light in the darkness.

Her faith was in Jesus Christ who was the source of her wisdom and strength. Like Paul in today's reading; as far as what
is important in life, she knew nothing "except Jesus Christ,
and him crucified." Her witness demonstrated the power of

the Holy Spirit, and it made a difference in how I felt about my work as a pastoral minister. She was a beacon of light working for justice. I knew there were many others like her. What if the many were to come together for justice for all, without regard to race, gender, social status, or religion?

At that time, St. Benedict Parish had become a member of the organization Metropolitan Organizing Strategy Enabling Strength (MOSES), a group of diverse congregations that organized communities, developed leaders, and built relationships to advocate for social justice. The pastor and parishioners were looking for ways to effectively use Catholic social thought to shed light on the different conditions under which people in the impoverished urban community lived, as well as those in the better-off neighborhoods surrounding the city. MOSES provided a venue to do just that.

The parish had a food pantry for those who were hungry and a flea market for those who needed clothes, but it wanted to do more than charity. Since the work of justice was a priority, those of us in the parish asked whether any of us were justified in keeping for his or her exclusive use what he or she did not need when others lacked necessities. From there we explored what could be done to transform human hearts to understand that all God's creation is for the common good. What did the universal destination of all created goods mean when it was obvious that in our parish there were many without the basic necessities of life while there were others who had more than they needed? What would it take to get those who possess goods to consider themselves administrators of the goods that God had entrusted to them?

Membership in MOSES gave parish members an opportunity to join with other faith-based communities from all over the metropolitan area, both wealthy and impoverished people, to find ways to transform human hearts toward the benefit of all in society. Together we explored an understanding of social development in the context of human solidarity. Our faith in Jesus Christ, the Redeemer, shed light in how human hearts can be freed from need and selfish attachment to wealth. We sought to discover what contributes to the growth of a new humanity that anticipates the world to come.

Concretely, members of MOSES sought equitable allocation and distribution of public funds, equal opportunities for quality public education, equal access to public transportation, equal opportunity for full and meaningful employment, and safe and healthy neighborhoods in which to live. The fair and just distribution of these opportunities would help us to be good administrators of the created goods God had given to all.

MOSES acted out of a belief in the truth Isaiah speaks of in the first reading: "If you offer your food to the hungry and satisfy the needs of the afflicted, then your light shall rise in the darkness and your gloom be like the noonday." Members of MOSES recognized the reality of social sin and the need for structural change, which is the work of justice.

Let us come to the table of the Eucharist today seeking forgiveness and liberation from our own selfishness and attachments to what we do not need. And when we are sent forth at the end of this celebration, let us act to satisfy the afflicted by working for structural change in obedience to the command of Christ: you must let your light shine before others, so that they may see your good works and give glory to your Father in heaven.

Sixth Sunday in Ordinary Time

Sr. Roni Schweyen, MM

Tanzania

Sirach 15:15–20; Psalm 119:1–2, 4–5, 17–18, 33–34;
First Corinthians 2:6–10; Matthew 5:17–37

If you choose, you can keep the commandments, and to act faithfully is a matter of your own choice.   —*Sirach 15:15*

In the reading from Sirach we hear that God has given us choices in our lives—to behave faithfully is within our power. Each day God grants us this ability to act in a faithful and just way. I would pose the question "How do we gain the strength to be faithful to God each day?" We can so easily be overcome by circumstances that take us away from the way of truth. In looking at the Gospels, we see Jesus amid the turmoil of his time. But he remained steadfast in his way of following peace. I would observe that he did so because he remained constant in his actions through a life of prayer. We remember hearing many times in the Gospels that Jesus went away to pray, and that he taught his apostles to pray. Thus, we in the modern world in our troubled milieu must also take time out to pray, to remain centered on what God wants for us and for the world.

The internationally renowned priest and author Henri Nouwen wrote in the book *Peacework: Prayer, Resistance, Community*: "Our prayer is a death to the world so that we can live for God." When we pray, it lifts us to know God's way for us. To the degree that we have divested ourselves and become free of fear, then we can act. It may be to work toward peace building, or to work for the rights of people who live in poor circumstances.

I lived for forty years in East Africa, where I worked with many Tanzanians who had to struggle against the economic conditions that kept them in poverty. Most Tanzanians even today live on about $1.50 per day; more often than not they have families to feed with this meager sum. I was humbled many times by their belief that God was helping them to live their faith.

When armed with love, Paul tells us, we are ambassadors for Christ. With respect to showing love to others, a Tanzanian woman named Emerenciana (Little Anna) is the best example I know. She became a counselor for AIDS patients in a small outreach ministry with which I worked in Tanzania. She found out that she was HIV positive, but she made the decision that she would live optimistically with the disease. She knew that she could reach out to help others who were HIV positive. Her husband became very angry that she was speaking out publicly. He beat her and chased her out of their home. She continued her work because she knew that she could be a positive difference for those who were so fearful of living with HIV and AIDS.

Emerenciana was a committed Christian. I saw her reach out to many people, even to those whom no one else would help. She continued her ministry to the sick for a number of years, helping others to live confidently and to be courageous in facing their future. She was able to begin and lead a group called "Women Living Positively with HIV and AIDS," with her love giving strength to others. Tragically, her life ended violently, yet her example of selflessness and dedication lives on in the lives of those she touched.

Paul wrote, "Love never ends" (First Corinthians 13:8), and when we love, we are free to choose the good and to decide to be on the side of justice. As Emerenciana chose to continue her work for those who were sick and marginalized, the example of her love for others does not die, but becomes even brighter as time goes on.

Seventh Sunday in Ordinary Time

Sr. Luise Ahrens, MM

Cambodia

Leviticus 19:1–2, 17–18; Psalm 103:1–4, 8, 10, 12–13;
First Corinthians 3:16–23; Matthew 5:38–48

And if anyone wants to sue you and take your coat, give your
cloak as well . . .   — *Matthew 5:40*

The first reading and the psalm today call us to love as God
loves: "You shall love your neighbor as yourself," and "As [a
parent] has compassion for his children, so the Lord has compassion for those who fear him." And this steadfast love of
God is, above all, universal; it is for every creature of God.

A few years ago, Gene LaVerdiere gave a retreat on scripture;
participants were asked one by one to read a section of Luke's
Christmas Gospel out loud: "There was no place for them in
the inn." We all remember that piece about Mary and Joseph
in Bethlehem, and how they could not find a place to stay
for the birth of Jesus. Then, Gene read the text himself, and
he read it with a difference: "There was no place for *them* in
the inn." The sense is completely changed, transformed—the
picture moves from crowded inns to a culture of not receiving
these "outsiders" into our place. He called us to look into our
hearts, to name the "thems" in our own lives, the people who
for us are "other." It was a serious and reflective time, one that
brought some people to tears as they thought about their own
issues of exclusion, of the need to put someone else down so
that they themselves appeared to be better, of the hidden but
real fear of those who seem different in some way, of the pain
we cause by body language that manifests the sin of exclusion.

In Cambodia, disabled people are generally put away in the back of the house, sometimes chained if their issues are mental illness or antisocial behavior. Until recently, there was even a law excluding disabled people from becoming teachers. In 2010, the first blind students entered the Royal University of Phnom Penh. They had been to a high school that was supervised by a group that specializes in teaching those who are blind or deaf, so it was a safe place for these young people. But the university is a different, scary place. It receives scholarship students from all over the country, so all of them are shy and uncertain in the beginning. When the new students arrived, as happens everywhere, the "cool kids" banded together, the others found friends, and the blind student, Sok Ang, was standing on the fringe of the group in the classroom, wanting to join in, but not knowing how.

This went on for a while until the teacher gathered the students together to talk, not wanting to point out difference, but rather seeking what was shared among all of them. She led them through a process in which each student wrote down what she or he wanted from university study, and then led them further in a reflective way to imagine life without legs, without arms, and then without eyes. . . . It was like a miniresurrection as all eyes turned to their blind companion, Sok Ang, and the light of their thoughtless and self-preserving cruelty dawned. They said almost as one: "Oh, teacher, he is like us inside." The Gospel came alive—if someone asks for your coat, give him your cloak as well—Sok Ang is always supported now, is walked from class to class, is read to and encouraged, and he in turn is a friend to all.

It is this gift we take from these readings today and which we can give each other—keep asking who are the "thems" in our own lives; who do we exclude, intentionally or not; who are chosen for groups, for gatherings, for friendship. Are we, each one of us, willing indeed, to "be holy [as] I the Lord your God am holy"?

Eighth Sunday in Ordinary Time

Marie Dennis, Maryknoll Affiliate

Washington, D.C.

Isaiah 49:14–15; Psalm 62:2–3, 6–7, 8–9; First Corinthians 4:1–5;
Matthew 6:24–34

*No one can serve two masters; for a slave will either hate the one
and love the other, or be devoted to the one and despise the other.*
—Matthew 6:24

After decades of civil war, as the possibility of peace in the
newly independent country of South Sudan seemed more real,
people began to return to the villages from which they had
fled and to think about the future.

"Therefore I tell you, do not worry about your life, what
you will eat or what you will drink, or about your body, what
you will wear. Is not life more than food, and the body more
than clothing?"

What could this admonition possibly mean to the people
of Bor or Nimule or Malakal or other South Sudanese communities when food security, access to water, land for grazing
their cattle or for farming, health care, basic education—even
passable roads—were far from certain? Perhaps it made more
sense to them than to those of us who thought security rested
on financial prowess, a successful career or many possessions,
and were bitterly disappointed to learn that having more
did not necessarily guarantee security when serious illness or
unemployment hit close to home. Western civilization's post
Enlightenment emphasis on individualism and post-Industrial
Revolution emphasis on material progress without concern
for the common good or the survival of the planet has left

us more vulnerable than secure. The size of the U.S. military budget makes that very clear.

For generations, the Sudanese and many African peoples have known that genuine security is nurtured in community. Perhaps the most devastating consequences of prolonged war in Sudan were the displacement of communities with the deep challenge that presents to sustained security, and the proliferation of small arms in local communities with the false sense of security they offer.

In Bor and Nimule and Malakal and in many other corners of the new South Sudan, people reclaimed life with hope and enormous creativity. As they began the long, challenging task of building a nation, they faced many important decisions about the future direction of their society. Would the development of South Sudan be shaped by external forces lusting for land and oil, profits and new markets? Would they be forced into an individualistic definition of development, or would they focus instead on the common good? Would they sustain right relationships with the natural world, with the corner of Mother Earth where they live, or would they adopt an economic model that is unsustainable? Would they find ways to rebuild security in local communities even as they rid themselves of the curse of small arms?

The Gospel message "You cannot serve God and wealth" and Catholic social (and environmental) teaching's measures of a moral economy can help us all imagine a future that is both sustainable and secure. In such a future, the global common good, vibrant local communities, and a good quality of life for all will take precedence over the accumulation of wealth and possessions by individuals or individual nations, diversity will be honored and protected, and weapons will be replaced by dialogue and diplomacy as tools for resolving international and intercommunity conflicts.

We live in a world that is intrinsically interconnected. How people living in consumer societies move into the future and how the people of South Sudan move into the future are of a piece. The international community can thrust South Sudan into the "real world" of competition for oil and land and water and markets, or we can accompany South Sudan respectfully on its own journey toward lasting peace and sustainability. If the ultimate goal is more for us, we will use every tool in the foreign policy tool kit (such as foreign aid, diplomacy, military might, economic persuasion) to help South Sudan open itself to western ideas and investment. If the ultimate goal is inclusive global security, we will listen with great care and help where we can as South Sudan cares for its own people and becomes the positive force in the Horn of Africa that its rich experience and diverse cultures have prepared it to become.

Ash Wednesday

Dave Kane, former Maryknoll lay missioner

Brazil; Maryknoll Office for Global Concerns

Joel 2:12–18; Psalm 51:3–6, 12–14, 17; Second Corinthians
5:20–6:2; Matthew 6:1–6, 16–18

Yet even now, says the Lord, return to me with all your heart,
with fasting, with weeping, and with mourning; rend your
hearts and not your clothing.   — *Joel 2:12–13a*

For nine years, starting in 1996, I lived and worked with
people in the city dump of João Pessoa, Brazil, on the eastern-
most point of the Americas. What was then a dump had once
been an unpolluted swamp. In the 1950s the city started to
throw its trash into the swamp and, after so many years, the
garbage had built up into a forty-acre island over a hundred
feet deep. Until 2003, when the city opened a new landfill,
hundreds of men, women, and children lived on top of that
island and sorted through the city's refuse as trucks poured
more than 750 tons of garbage into the swamp every day.
Whether under the brutally hot sun during the dry season, or
slugging through knee-high mud, they worked long hours to
earn minimal incomes.

As Maryknoll missioners around the world can attest, scenes
like this, true social and ecological nightmares, are repeated in
nearly every country of the world. Abject poverty is not a reality for a tiny portion of the human family but for huge swaths
of the population. In every country where Maryknollers work,
ecological destruction is also expanding at a rapid pace.

I think the reality of the dump/swamp in João Pessoa
encapsulates well the two most prominent reasons why we are

in need of Ash Wednesday's call for repentance: As a human family, we have become unaware of, and insensitive to, how our actions and lifestyles contribute to the destruction of both God's creation and human dignity. We fail to acknowledge how we are active participants in a system that strangles all forms of life with toxins and pollution while forcing hundreds of millions of people to go to bed hungry.

It is crucial that we remember that everything that we buy and use is made of something extracted from earth and processed by human workers. Our consumption directly implies the destruction and removal of parts of earth's bounty.

To help remember the effects of our consumption, it may help to recall scenes of human and environmental damage caused by the production of the things we use every day. When you drive your car, think of scenes from the BP Deepwater Horizon oil catastrophe in the Gulf of Mexico, or Chevron and Texaco's destruction of the Ecuadoran Amazon. Let those images sear into your memory. Have you ever bought gasoline from those companies? I know I have.

If you eat chicken, beef, or pork, it is more than likely that the meat you are consuming comes from animals raised and killed in what's known as a "confined animal feeding operation." As you eat, envision scenes from these horrific places. Remember that this reality—animals, created and loved by God, forced into unimaginable suffering during their short lives—exists in order to provide cheap meat for us.

Our constant search for cheaper products pushes corporate leaders to search for places where they can pay the lowest wages and pollute most freely in order to lower costs. We often blame corporate CEOs for their rapacious actions without recognizing that they are responding to our own demands. We are all a fundamental part in this process.

The concept of repentance is not an easy one for many people. We like to focus on the positive, on the promise of the Easter Resurrection, instead of dwelling on Ash Wednesday's call for repentance or the suffering of Good Friday. But in order to truly resurrect into a new way of living and acting, we need to first acknowledge our failings and the part we play in the human and environmental suffering we see around us.

This Ash Wednesday, let's stay in the uncomfortable space of repentance. Let's not jump to the Resurrection, but take advantage of the wisdom of this holy day to reflect on the role we play in this destruction and consider what changes we can make in our lives to help restore humanity and earth.

How do I spend my money? Does my money support life or death? Does my investment fund chase the largest profits with the most destructive businesses or does it sustain healthy livelihoods and ecologically responsible business practices? How do I use my time? Do I spend more time contributing to the planet's human and ecological wounds or to healing them? How can I change my actions and lifestyle to be more in tune with God's plan for the world?

First Sunday of Lent

Sr. Janet Hockman, MM

Nepal

Genesis 2:7–9, 3:1–7; Psalm 51:3–6; 12–14, 17; Romans 5:12–19; Matthew 4:1–11

Restore to me the joy of your salvation, and sustain in me a willing spirit.   —*Psalm 51:12*

Ashes have surely gone from our foreheads by now. How long did they help us to remember oneness with the earth and all humanity, to turn from sin and believe, to follow the ways of Jesus, cross included, as prevailing love?

How long ago, or recently, were we wet with waters of baptism, knowing that strength and confidence of one in whom God is well pleased? When was a time of fasting and prayer distilling the disposition of our hearts, humbly acknowledging what hungers mask and clarify? Who and what do we trust to bear us up? What tempts us toward appealing and seemingly comfortable powerful and privileged positions? When do we deem them possible to propose to and impose on others? When are we led and when do we lead ourselves into temptation? And when are we graced to see occasions of temptation clarifying our relationship with God, with each other, and as sharers of the universe?

A gentle image comes to me: a child's chubby hand placed on my cheek, turning my face for attention. Distractions are not tolerated! It may be a playful gesture, but the message is clear: Turn. Look here. See and engage! Isn't the message similar in this time of Lent? Out of tiredness and hunger, look at the realities around us; believe we are called and sent and sustained by God's love; with passion instead of possessiveness, open a wide heart of love and hope for well-being to all that is within and before us.

With the background of today's Gospel, I took a glance to places of seeing stones that exposed hungers. From the day I arrived in Nepal, I knew the importance of the Bagmati River. I walked a bridge across the river five days a week for months. Along its shore were tent cities alive with homeless and displaced persons who depended on the river's flow for food and cleansing. The waters also received the ashes of the dead cremated along the banks, carrying spirits into a new life. The river swelled with seasonal rains my first two years there. Then the stench was no longer flushed with flowing waters. The river was running dry. River stones caught tons of trash. The days of watching people perched on rocks to fish were no more. Remembering the river flow alone won't cover those stones again or feed the hungry at the shore. It's tempting to be overwhelmed with the spread of illnesses among the bank-dwellers, knowing the children there are unschooled, and being aware of ecological issues of water pollution.

Basically one road runs into and out of the Kathmandu Valley. There is always traffic congestion; departure and arrival times can rarely be planned. The vistas are breathtaking and life-taking. The road is full of switchbacks and kilometers without guardrails warning of steep cliff drop-offs. Landslides and mudslides rumble and tumble unthwarted. Erosion follows the loss of trees to firewood and charcoal and to timber taken for export furniture industries. Ancient pathways have new detours. How does a nation trust its well-being to the hands of consumer societies, those who can afford it by pay or prodding? What wise ones will plan and replant and stabilize hold the earth?

It's hard to get much higher on this earth than the top of the Himalayan Mountains. Its peaks have been reached by sherpas and climbers for years. They are panoramic places; surely it seems impossible to take it all in. Yet there are political borders below. Refugees have fled, people have been exiled, visitors have become unwelcomed, and boundaries and ethnic identities are in dispute. Who has ever really had the right to take possession of land? Global warming has already met the mountains. What will it take to melt temptations of political possessiveness and hostilities also in our times? How can any of us see that far from wherever we are? How do we look and see as God sees? How do we look through the eyes of Jesus?

We seldom plan to get stopped in the middle of things, to begin something new or again in the middle. Lent began in the middle, in the middle of a week. In the middle of life, can we pay attention to deepest hungers? Can we acknowledge times and presentations of temptations while trusting in God's love and that very love being entrusted to us? Can we look again at the ways we project needs, use powers and privileges? Can we envision the melting of fears to reveal newness and renewal of the face of the earth?

Second Sunday of Lent

Charlotte Cook, former Maryknoll lay missioner

Kenya

Genesis 12:1–4; Psalm 33:4–5, 18–20, 22; Second Timothy1:8–10;
Matthew 17:1–9

*Truly the eye of the Lord is on those who fear him, on those who
hope in his steadfast love, to deliver their soul from death, and
to keep them alive in famine.* —Psalm 33:18–19

We read in today's passage from Genesis, "The Lord said to
Abram, 'Go from your country and your kindred and your
father's house to the land that I will show you.'" We know
that "Abram went, as the Lord had told him." It must have
been extremely difficult for him to cut himself off from his
native land and his people to go to some unknown place. Africans can appreciate the sacrifice that Abram made because they
too have strong attachments to their homelands.

Land has a different significance for Africans than it has for
people in the United States. I came to understand these differences while I worked in Kenya. Land in sub-Saharan Africa
connects the people to their place of origin. Land keeps the
members of an ethnic group together. Land is security; it is
wealth; it is home. Land is the inheritance for future generations. Africans believe that their land itself is sacred because it
was given to them by God. I knew Kenyans who swallowed a bit
of Kenyan soil—in order to remain connected to their land and
home—before leaving the country to study or to work abroad.

Land has been a source of conflict in Kenya since colonial
times. However, recent years have seen an increase in assaults
on the sanctity of the land. I witnessed these changes and saw

how devastating this ecological degradation is to the people. Who has been most affected by these shifts in land use? The small farmers and others who rely on the land for their livelihoods have been the hardest hit.

Ethnic clashes, often politically motivated, have forced people off their land, and in the ensuing violence, homes, businesses, and crops have been destroyed. When people are forced to relocate, land is left unfarmed, reducing people's incomes and the availability of food in the region. In the past, people who were violently chased off in ethnic conflict were often targeted again and forced to settle in displaced persons camps or to relocate a third time to another part of the country just for belonging to the "wrong" ethnic group.

Today only 8 percent of Kenya's land is arable. Practices like cutting trees for cooking fuel leads to deforestation and land desertification. This brings on an increase in landslides, lowers rainfall levels, decreased watershed areas, and an increase in drought. Parts of Kenya, especially in the north, are almost always dry, forcing pastoralists to wander in search of good pasture for their livestock. In this search for grazing resources and water, one community often encroaches on the land and wells of another. Violence between neighboring ethnic groups is not uncommon. During times of severe drought it was not unusual to see Maasai people bringing their herds of cattle to downtown Nairobi to graze on whatever grass they could find.

Another challenge is the increasing difficulty of subdividing farms for future generations. When farm plots become too small, farmers cannot sufficiently feed their families. If small farmers have a surplus to sell, they now compete with large industrialized farms with the best farm equipment and fertilizers, or with imported grains that are often sold below the cost of production. Large industrialized farms not only have the means to irrigate, they also wield political power to ensure that national policies add to their profits.

Cut flowers have become an important export from Kenya. Large flower farms now surround Lake Naivasha using the lake as a source of water for irrigation. The high water demand of the cut-flower industry has lowered the lake's water table and negatively affected small farmers and the people who fish in the lake. Under these circumstances, people, especially the youth, leave the rural area to find work in the cities. Millions of Kenyans now live in urban slums and have no access to land to grow their own food, and insufficient income to buy adequate food for a healthy diet.

My experience in Kenya gave me an understanding of the importance of the land for Kenyans, as well as the life-and-death consequences that result from not treating the land with care. Now that I have returned to the United States, I think about land very differently. I try to be mindful how my actions affect land use and abuse around the world. Land is a gift from God. I continually challenge myself with the following questions: Do I support fair trade products that benefit the small farmers? Do I teach others to connect the dots between our lifestyles here and the land in Kenya?

Third Sunday of Lent

Br. Mark Gruenke, MM

Brazil; Mozambique; Namibia

Exodus 17:3–7; Psalm 95:1–2, 6–9; Romans 5:1–2, 5–8;
John 4:5–42 or 4:5–15, 19–26, 39–42

*The Samaritan woman said to him, "How is it that you, a Jew,
ask a drink of me, a woman of Samaria?" (Jews do not share
things in common with Samaritans).* —John 4:9

Jesus was hot and tired. The sun was burning down directly
overhead. He was resting by a well. The disciples had gone off
in search of food. Jesus was in a foreign country among people
who had different beliefs and customs from his own.

A single woman drew near with a vessel to fetch water. We
ask why she would come alone and in the middle of the day
rather than in the early morning or in the late afternoon when
all the other women normally go for water. It makes us wonder
if she is not perhaps the village outcast. But for Jesus there are
no outcasts. He speaks to her, acknowledging her presence
and admitting his own thirst. He reaches across the divide
between two peoples. The woman is astounded. There seems
to be rebuke in her voice when she questions his disregard for
the long-standing enmity between two peoples and the way he
boldly breaks gender taboos common to both cultures. How
can a Jew ask the help of a Samaritan and, worse yet, a strange
man speak to her, a woman to whom he is not related?

But Jesus is not one to let this special moment pass by.
Her appeal to old prejudices and taboos does not merit his
response. He immediately invites this Samaritan woman to
enter into a discussion with him. He urges her to look beyond

her own cultural restrictions and limitations to see the deeper
spiritual truth that he represents. She challenges him in return.
Does he dare to suggest that he is greater than her ances-
tor Jacob? Jesus' response is blunt. The water from Jacob's
well temporarily quenches bodily thirst, but what Jesus offers
will fulfill spiritual needs. The woman either is not willing to
accept Jesus' claim to be greater than Jacob or she simply does
not understand what he is offering her, for her response seems
to be quite flippant. Can we even hear some sarcasm in her
remark that if she had some of Jesus' water she would never
have to make the long, lonely trip to the well again?

If there is any sarcasm, Jesus ignores it; instead he hears the
pain that she suffers as an outcast. He doesn't take offense
in what could be taken as a belittling response, but he goes
directly to the issue of her marital status. She has engaged in
socially unacceptable behavior, which apparently has caused
her to be isolated within her own community. She is clearly
impressed by Jesus' knowledge of this painful history of hers
and is touched by his concern. Opening herself to serious dialogue, she begins to show a much deeper interest in what he
has to say. Because Jesus has broken the communication bar-
rier between Jew and Samaritan the woman feels emboldened
to go right to the central religious dispute between these two
peoples: Is God to be worshipped on the mountain in Samaria
or in the Temple in Jerusalem? But her question is one that
treats of the externals of religion.

Jesus refuses to stay at that level; he calls her to a more
intense level. He reminds her that God is spirit. Jesus declares,
and he seems to do so with some passion, that worship of God
is not centered in externals but that it must be grounded in
spirit. The woman appears to grasp the truth in what Jesus
is saying. She, in turn, reveals her own deep longing for the

Messiah to make everything clear. Jesus, moved by her openness, gives this outcast Samaritan woman the great honor of
being one of the few in the Gospels to whom he directly reveals
himself. He declares to her that he is the Messiah. The woman
sets her jar down, perhaps a symbol of the heavy oppression
that she has carried all these years, and hurries to the village
to announce to all that the Messiah has come. The villagers
invite Jesus to stay with them. Jesus stays with them two days.
At first, they welcome him because of the woman's testimony.
Later, they believe in him because they themselves have come
to know Jesus.

Today's Gospel reveals clearly the dynamic of foreign mission. Leaving one's home and going to minister in a strange
land to an unfamiliar people is not easy. The missionary is often
not well received when he or she first arrives. The missionary is
a foreigner. Who invited him or her to come anyway?

The missionary must embody certain key attitudes in order
to be faithful to his or her task. Jesus shows us how to approach
the other in a respectful manner. He sets aside all prejudices of
class, ethnicity, and even of religion to reach out to the other
as a person of dignity, deserving of respect. He seems to seek
out those who are most marginalized within society. He seeks
opportunities to initiate dialogue with the other, always taking the other seriously. He hears not only the words that they
speak but what lies behind their words. He notes any incon-
gruity between words and actions. He is not afraid in the least
to show his own humanity. Jesus' number-one motivation is
not his own personal justification but the welfare of the other.

Because Jesus does not erect defenses, neither for himself
nor for his message, others are encouraged to lower their own
defenses and to trust in him. Conversation with Jesus does not
happen at the superficial level. Jesus seems to go immediately

to the heart of the matter. Jesus' approach is nonjudgmental. Sinners experience God's forgiveness through their contact with Jesus. He shares the lifestyle of the people with whom he ministers. He eats their food and drinks their water. He places himself completely at the mercy of their generosity to meet his basic needs for food, water, and lodging.

When the Samaritans invite him, he is willing to live with them in their homes for two days. As Jesus touches the hearts of the individuals whom he encounters, they are energized to carry his message to their own families and neighbors and even, perhaps, across borders. At first, the people whom these witnesses contact are attracted by their words and actions but eventually, as those contacted begin to know Jesus, it is their relationship with Jesus that becomes of paramount importance to them.

As a Maryknoll missionary I have experienced in my own life the missionary dynamic that today's Gospel recounts. But I have discovered that there is a beautiful twist to it. Even though we go out officially as missionaries in the name of the church, it is Jesus, through the action of the Spirit, who is truly the missionary. To be in mission is to enter into a relationship with others that is totally governed by the Holy Spirit. We missionaries are as much transformed by our experience as are those to whom we are sent. Just as others meet Jesus through our ministry, we too, meet Jesus who is present when two or three meet in his name. It is a most wonderful experience. Can anyone imagine anything of greater value for which to dedicate one's life?

Even though we try to copy Jesus' way of being in mission, we do not become Jesus, the missionary. Rather, we are tools of the Spirit. It is still Jesus today, through the power of the Holy Spirit, who is doing the mission work. Both those who receive the missionary and the one who is sent are ministered to by Jesus. Paul says it very clearly elsewhere in the scriptures when he says, "It is no longer I who live, but it is Christ who lives in me" (Galatians 2:20). Neither you nor I can bring salvation to anyone else. Only Jesus saves. We can be his instruments. We can be sent as missionaries to another country and to another people. We can give of ourselves in compassionate service, meeting the needs of others by building a parish or doing works of mercy or of justice. But it is through the relationships that we establish while on mission that Jesus, through the Spirit, does the actual mission. Jesus transforms both the one sent in mission as well as those who receive the missionary. This is the heart of mission. The woman at the well carried the message of Jesus to her village. It is precisely because she was transformed by Jesus that the other villagers were willing to accept Jesus and be transformed by his presence in their own lives.

Missionaries agree to be sent, to be used by the Spirit. And our reward, if we are faithful, is to be changed by the missionary action of Jesus, who is present in our ministry. We seek to experience the transforming power of the Holy Spirit present when we reach out to others in Jesus' name. This presence seems to be a universal experience for all missionaries. Ask any missionary and he or she will respond, "I receive much more than I give in mission." And it is a truthful statement, not just feigned humility on his or her part. Within the missionary's ministry, Jesus, through the Spirit, is at work transforming all parties, the one who was sent as well as the ones who have welcomed him or her.

Fourth Sunday of Lent

Angel Mortel, former Maryknoll lay missioner

Brazil

First Samuel 16:1, 6–7, 10–13; Psalm 23; Ephesians 5:8–14;
John 9:1–41 or 9:1, 6–9, 13–17, 34–38

Do not look on his appearance or on the height of his stature,
because I have rejected him; for the Lord does not see as mortals
see; they look on the outward appearance, but the Lord looks on
the heart.   —First Samuel 16:7

In today's Gospel, the disciples ask Jesus whose sin caused the man's blindness, and Jesus says he is blind so that God's power might be seen at work in him. Often we look at challenging situations and wonder: Why? How could this be? What went wrong? As a missioner in Brazil, I lived and worked with many people who were excluded, forgotten, poor, and sickly, and my thoughts were mostly focused on the injustice of the situation. I often overlooked the positive healing power of God working through these situations.

In São Paulo, I worked mainly with community health workers, or leaders, as we called them. Most of the leaders lived in the resource-poor communities where we worked and were very familiar with the conditions. We accompanied families that had children who were at risk of malnutrition or disease related to poor nutrition. Most of these children lived in extreme poverty. The leaders followed the physical and social development of each child through regular visits, offered nutritional advice, checked to see that vaccines were up-to-date and helped parents gain access to social services.

Izanete was a committed and creative leader. She joined our team with much hesitation. Her husband had told her that her only responsibility in life was to take care of him, her kids, and their home. She believed him until we invited her to participate in our work and to share her many gifts with the larger community. Izanete was timid at first, but was soon visiting several families and having a positive impact on her local community. I will always remember her for her ability to bring people together. In one very specific case she helped to open the eyes of the community to a group of children and families who were sadly forgotten and excluded.

During her monthly visits to families, Izanete would stop at every shack in one narrow passageway of the shantytown, except for one. She asked the other mothers who lived there if there were any children in that shack. They said, "Oh yes, but stay away from that house." Their reaction revealed great fear of what lay behind those closed doors. There is too much pain in that house, they said. They never talked to the young woman who lived there or her "strange child."

Izanete thought that was exactly where she needed to be. So she knocked on the door. The house was all closed up and quiet. No one answered the door, but Izanete insisted. Finally a young and sickly young woman came to the door. Izanete introduced herself and said she had heard that a young child lived there. She described her work in the community and asked if she could meet the child. The woman flatly said no. Izanete insisted, sensing that there was a story to be heard. Eventually she convinced the woman, who turned out to be the mother of the child, to let her in.

There she met a tiny, five-year-old girl in diapers lying on the floor in the corner of a dark room. The girl drooled and grunted as Izanete bent down to say hello. The mother began to tell a tragic story of an unwanted pregnancy, of hospital errors, of a child born with brain damage, and of total rejection from family and neighbors. The mother lived depressed and isolated in her house, hiding in shame from the judgment and jeers of society.

Slowly, Izanete developed a deep friendship with the mother, whose name was Rita. Izanete gained Rita's trust by telling her own story of feeling shame and hiding in her house. She encouraged Rita to get out of her house and meet the neighbors. Their first encounters were awkward, but the fear of the other slowly dissipated with contact. Soon the neighbors were sharing stories of other families they knew who had children with disabilities.

Izanete came up with the idea of bringing together all those families and others in the community to create a support group for families with disabled children. This group became a huge success and eventually made more visible the presence of these families in the community. The group not only served as support for each of its members, but they also advocated on behalf of disabled children and their families and helped others in the community better understand their challenges. The group raised money for wheelchairs for kids who needed them, petitioned for their right to special transportation, and learned more about special programs for people with disabilities.

In today's first reading, God chose David to be the next king not on outward appearances, but by "look[ing] on the heart." And God chose Izanete, the unlikely leader, to bring together a community that was divided by fear—fear of the other, the unknown, the different. She called people to live in the light, to open the doors of their closed hearts and believe as we heard in Ephesians that "the fruit of the light is found in all that is good and right and true." And it is through a little excluded five-year-old girl and her mother that the community experienced the healing power of God.

Fifth Sunday of Lent

Marj Humphrey, former Maryknoll lay missioner

Kenya

Ezekiel 37:12–14; Psalm 130; Romans 8:8–11; John 11:1–45

Thus says the Lord God: I am going to open your graves, and bring you up from [them] . . . I will put my spirit within you, and you shall live.   *—Ezekiel 37:12–14*

I am the resurrection and the life. Those who believe in me, even though they die, will live, and everyone who lives and believes in me will never die. Do you believe this?   *—John 11:25–26*

We have begun the last week in Lent, and the readings today heighten our anticipation of the Resurrection. We have done our best to sacrifice, to pray, to reflect on our weaknesses, and now we anticipate the Resurrection.

And yet, aren't most "resurrections" unanticipated? The joy, the awe coming from great and unexpected things? We teach our children, grandchildren, students, about life, death, and resurrection through gardens, through planting seeds for school projects. And we delight in their surprise at seeing an unexpected form of life burst forth for the first time. We mourn the loss of an elder, feel palpable grief and sorrow, only to be caught off guard by a new birth in the family, or a wedding, that suddenly brings unexpected balm to our wound. Or we are given a surprising insight, in the midst of everyday life, through a person from an altogether other culture and belief.

A number of years ago, while I was working as a Maryknoll lay missioner health care worker in Kenya, a young couple brought their infant twins to our hospital. One infant was critically ill, barely alive from the ravages of meningitis. The second twin, fortunately, was in very early stages of the disease. I was quite certain the first child would not live through the night, but equally as certain that the second infant, with proper treatment, would survive. I did my best to prepare the parents for this, quite grateful that the husband spoke fairly good English and I could express myself with the necessary nuances rather than try to do this in my fledgling and broken Swahili. I was afraid that after the dying infant passed away, they would no longer believe in our medicine and refuse further treatment for the other baby.

As expected, the first infant died that night, in the arms of his devoted mother. And indeed, my worst fears were realized when the father came to ask for the body of his child, and also asking me to discharge the other child from the hospital. I did my best to dissuade him, arrogantly assuming he did not understand, explaining over and over again about antibiotics, the science of disease, the need to keep the child in hospital. The man quietly but firmly persisted.

Exasperated, I finally burst out, "But you don't understand! If you leave here you will have two dead children, instead of one. How can you do this to your child?" (To this day I am still ashamed of my outburst.) The young man looked kindly at me and said in a gentle voice, "No, you are the one who does not understand. You see, it is our belief that if the twin of someone who has died is not present at the burial of his twin, that person's spirit cannot be released to the ancestors. I believe this is what you, in your faith, call 'heaven.' His soul will be trapped forever in the grave, and he will never enjoy life with the ancestors. How can I do that to my child?"

The purity and clarity of his belief in afterlife rendered me, the missioner, silent. Many years later, I still ponder this. His absolute certainty in the resurrection, of the need to live out his beliefs so that his child could be raised up, humbles me to this day.

Resurrection is life . . . and mystery. The story of the twins is complex and gives me more questions than answers. Some ethnic groups of Kenya believe that the afterlife of an individual, their "resurrected life," is actually their children living on in this world. Likewise, among many, there is a strong sense of the living dead, a belief that the ancestors are alive and well, still present among us, though no longer visible in the body. One of my favorite traditions in Kenya is the ritual first drink at family gatherings. Before a celebration can begin, the first drink is dipped out of the communal pot and poured into the ground "for the ancestors." It says, "You are here with us. You still live among us. You are still living, you have not died!"

I carry these experiences with me into our own celebration of the Resurrection. My reflections on these images—that of dried seeds blossoming into new life, our children as some sense of our resurrection, our ancestors as the living dead to be revered—bring many questions. How can we better safeguard our earth so that generations of children who come after us may live on in the glory of creation? Will our libations for the ancestors be tainted with the blood of our wars and violence against others, or tainted with our unfettered greed or blind prejudice toward those with whom we live our daily lives? Or will we honor them with lives of goodness and justice?

Belief in the Resurrection presents us with the challenges that Christ gave us through his own life of service, his sacrifices, his dying to self. It is a holy challenge and a passionate challenge. We have rich symbolism awaiting us: the paschal fire—the light that banishes darkness and gives light to our paths, the fire that gives life.

I offer you a prayer of the Maasai people of Kenya and Tanzania:

> Receive this holy fire.
> Make your lives like this fire,
> A holy life that is seen,
> A life that has no end,
> A life that darkness does not overcome.
> May this light of God in you grow.
> Light a fire that is worthy of your heads.
> Light a fire that is worthy of your children.
> Light a fire that is worthy of your fathers.
> Light a fire that is worthy of your mothers.
> Now go in peace.
> May the Almighty protect you
> today and all days.

Palm Sunday

Sr. Antoinette Gutzler, MM

Taiwan

Isaiah 50:4–7; Psalm 22:8–9, 17–20, 23–24; Philippians 2:6–11;
Matthew 26:14–27, 66 or 27:11–54

> *. . . but emptied himself, taking the form of a slave, being*
> *born in human likeness. And being found in human form, he*
> *humbled himself and became obedient . . .* —*Philippians 2:7*

The readings of this Palm Sunday lead each Christian believer
into the mystery, challenge, and implications of Holy Week.
Isaiah speaks of the fidelity of the prophet and the consequences of speaking as God speaks. Philippians draws us into
the kenosis of Jesus—the call to leave one's comfort zone and
empty one's heart and life of all that is not of the divine. Matthew's Gospel propels us into the horror of the powerlessness
of the victim before the powers that be and the torture and
suffering of crucifixion. What must we speak, what must we
empty, and what are the consequences of these actions? What
must we suffer?

In March 2011, the world watched creation groaning and
the Japanese people suffering from the 9.0 earthquake that
struck off the northern coast of Japan. We witnessed the after-
math of the tsunami—villages wiped out, family, friends, livelihood all gone—and the day-to-day living with the reality of
damaged nuclear reactors and all that entails. Other reports
told of massive suffering through climate change in reports
of unprecedented flooding, deforestation, earthquakes,
typhoons, and political tensions around the globe. Truly creation is groaning.

Within the past few years, Pope John Paul II and Pope-Benedict XVI have called for response to the earth's groaning. In prescient words, John Paul II spoke of the need for an "ecological conversion," for "if one looks at the regions of our planet, one realizes immediately that humanity has disappointed the divine expectation." The theme of Pope Benedict XVI's 2010 New Year's address—"If you want to cultivate peace, protect creation"—emphasized that "respect for creation is of immense consequence not least because 'creation is the beginning and foundation of all God's works.'" He then addressed the reality of our inhumanity to one another through wars, conflicts, terrorism, and violation of human rights, and our misuse of the earth and the natural goods God has given us.

In that light, we can reflect on Matthew's Gospel as a challenge to our awareness of what we must choose between in terms of an ecological conversion. In bringing Jesus before the crowd, Pilate gives the people a choice: who do they want, Jesus or Barabbas? On this Palm Sunday, we contrast these two and perhaps see ourselves in the choice the people make. It is clear that Barabbas is a criminal; Jesus is a preacher of the Reign of God. Barabbas is possibly a man of some violence while Jesus is the nonviolent victim who stands in the place of all those harmed by violence against all living things. Barabbas stands for the status quo. He represents what we know and do even if we know it is or can be harmful to us.

The modern-day choice for Barabbas is a choice to harm the environment and to protect our national and world securities through the building of armaments over the way of life that God has given us in creation. In contrast, Jesus brings something new. He embodies the riskiness of the Reign of God that we are not sure we want, even though we need it desperately. He calls us to enter his kenosis in the desire to empty oneself. It is a movement from self-interest to concern and action for the common good. It is a movement from what is good for me, as a society, country, or nation, to what is the common good for all on earth. It is a prophetic courage that speaks to a weary world what it does not want to hear.

Palm Sunday can teach us about the reality of who we truly are. The choice before us is clear: the status quo—the world as it is, including all its forms of violence—or the world as it could be if God were really in charge.

Who do you choose: Jesus or Barabbas?

Holy Thursday Mass of the Lord's Supper

Sr. Helen Graham, MM

Philippines

Exodus 12:1–8, 11–14; Psalm 116:12–13, 15–18;
First Corinthians 11:23–26; John 13:1–15

This day shall be a day of remembrance for you. You shall celebrate it as a festival to the Lord; throughout your generations you shall observe it as a perpetual ordinance. —Exodus:12:14

The Second Vatican Council has restored to prominence the Easter Vigil and the Triduum, which begins Holy Thursday evening. Several rich themes dominate the liturgy of Holy Thursday evening. All of the readings focus on a sacred meal: Pesach, Eucharist, and the Last Supper. Meals are very significant in most cultures, and meals involve a diversity of food preparations expressive of cultural diversity.

Diversity is the watchword of the Institute of Formation and Religious Studies (IFRS) where I teach sacred scripture. Roughly half the student population, mostly sisters, but also brothers, priests, and laypeople, come from at least eleven Asian countries and even from Congo and Haiti, making our institute a living witness to the God of Israel, the God of all the nations who calls each one by name. Eating together and enjoying the rich cultural diversity in food and dress represented by our students is profoundly enriching and leads to a great sense of solidarity and appreciation among us.

It is in the context of a meal that the identity story of Israel, the story of the Exodus, is rehearsed and passed on from one generation to the next through the reading of the Haggadah at the annual Passover celebration in Jewish households around the world. Our first reading provides the ritual background for this meal, focusing particularly on the Passover lamb. The reading from Paul speaks of handing on to the community that that he received, i.e., the Eucharistic ritual that in its origins was also a meal, either a Passover meal (as in the Synoptic tradition) or a meal that took place the day before Passover as the lambs were being sacrificed (the Johannine tradition), and that took on Passover significance in the early community.

The Gospel portion provides the atmosphere of Jesus' final meal with his disciples during which the most profound symbolic action and conversation takes place. Unfortunately, the usual Holy Thursday overliteral practice of the priest humbly washing feet obscures, in a way, the really profound meaning of this sign. If one does a careful and close reading of the exchange between Jesus and Peter, it is clear that something eminently more solemn is operating here than Peter's refusal to allow his teacher to perform the humble physical service of washing his feet:

> "Lord, are you going to wash my feet?" Jesus answered, "You do not know now what I am doing, but later you will understand." Peter said to him, "You will never wash my feet." Jesus answered, "Unless I wash you, you have no share with me." Simon Peter said to him, "Lord, not my feet only but also my hands and my head!" (John 13:6–9)

A clue is provided in the introduction to the second part of the fourth Gospel, which also introduces chapter 13: Jesus knew that his hour had come to depart from this world and go to the Father. Having loved his own who were in the world, he loved them to the end. The Greek word used here can mean also "ultimately." And ultimate love, as Jesus says later in the

Gospel, is to lay down one's life for one's friends (John 15:13; cf. 13:34). In this foot-washing scene, Jesus is symbolizing his coming death. Jesus "took off his outer robe," equivalent to his life; and after having washed their feet he once again "put on his robe," i.e., his life, and said to them:

> "Do you know what I have done to you? You call me Teacher and Lord—and you are right, for that is what I am. So if I, your Lord and Teacher, have washed your feet, you also ought to wash one another's feet. For I have set you an example, that you also should do as I have done to you."

Sandra Schneiders makes this insightful note in her commentary on this scene, "Peter's adamant resistance to what Jesus was doing can be seen now in a very different light. . . . Peter understands more than he articulates. . . . Peter's refusal of Jesus' act of service was equivalent, then, to a rejection of the death of Jesus, understood as the laying down of his life for those he loved, and implying a radically new order of human relationships" ["The Foot Washing (John 13:1–20)," *Catholic Biblical Quarterly*, January 1981].

The sacred meals that we commemorate at this Eucharistic celebration remind us that Jesus has given his life for all humankind and that as we come together in our cultural diversity, our own meals also share in that sacred quality. How do we carry forth the example given to us by Jesus?

Grateful for the reality we celebrate during this Triduum, culminating in Easter, we pray with the psalmist:

What shall I return to the Lord
for all his bounty to me?

I will lift up the cup of salvation
and call on the name of the Lord,

I will pay my vows to the Lord
in the presence of all his people. . . .
I will offer to you a thanksgiving sacrifice
and call on the name of the Lord.

(Psalm 116:12–14, 17)

Good Friday

Sr. Roni Schweyen, MM

Tanzania

Isaiah 52:13–53:12; Psalm 31:2, 6, 12–13, 15–16, 17, 25;
Hebrews 4:14–16, 5:7–9; John 18:1–19:42

Although he was a Son, he learned obedience through what he suffered; and having been made perfect, he became the source of eternal salvation for all who obey him . . .   —Hebrews 4:8–9

Good Friday is a day of prayer and remembrance for Christians, and on this day we as Christians are faced with suffering in its starkest form. In the reading from Isaiah, we read of the suffering servant, which is the fourth oracle from Isaiah that predicts—more than six hundred years before Jesus was born—how God's faithful servant will endure pain at the hands of others and die. It is this suffering servant that we see as being fulfilled in the life of Jesus: "But he was wounded for our transgressions, crushed for our iniquities; upon him was the punishment that made us whole. . . . The Lord has laid on him the iniquity of us all."

Other foreshadowing in the Gospels points to Jesus' future life. In the Gospel of Luke, Simeon prophesies when he meets Jesus and his parents in the Temple, telling Mary that her child will be a sign of contradiction to many; a sword of sorrow will pierce her heart. Simeon's words, so mysterious to her, also apply to Christians in that they will also have sorrow and suffering because of their choice to follow Jesus.

Like Mary, we may ask, why did Jesus submit to the cruelties inflicted upon him by the soldiers and those in power who condemned him? Early Christians struggled with this question, and in the reading from Hebrews the author states that Jesus "learned obedience through what he suffered."

Working with HIV and AIDS patients for twelve years in Tanzania, I saw the suffering that whole families go through when a member is HIV positive. Francis was a thirty-eight-year-old man who had gone to the capital, Dar es Salaam, where he worked in the police force. He contracted AIDS, and when he became very weak, he returned to his family home in Nyakato. His mother and father were subsistence farmers with only a meager plot of land. During the time that Francis was sick, they sacrificed and used the small amount of money that they had for his medicines and his care.

When I first met Francis he was very bitter and blamed God for his sickness. I saw over a period of two years how Francis struggled with suffering as he developed a fungus, which began on his feet and spread to his legs. He eventually could not walk because the sores on the bottom of his feet became too painful. In Tanzania it was nearly impossible to get the proper medicines. In struggling with the pain, and also with the knowledge that he would not get better, Francis said, "You know, Jesus suffered for three days, but I'm here in bed suffering for over a year!" Slowly Francis came to grips with his anger. Before his death, Francis accepted his suffering, and he died in peace, reconciled with God.

In John's Gospel, Jesus says: "Am I not to drink the cup that the Father has given me?" In saying these words to Peter, who had picked up his sword and defended Jesus, Jesus shows us that he accepts the Creator's will for him. Sometimes our resistance is in the form of nonacceptance, like that of Francis, and at other times we violently resist what is required of us. But the use of the sword is not the way of Jesus. Violence only begets violence, and he has chosen the other—the way of nonviolence, the way of love.

The Passion is known to us in its details, and each time that it is read another truth may be revealed. The mystery is still there, but the life, death, and the Resurrection of Jesus expose us to the real meaning of our journey. This salvation story, how Jesus accepted his cross, gives us the basic meaning for our journey through life. In this way of the cross, Jesus was reconciling the whole world to himself.

Easter Sunday

Marie Dennis, Maryknoll Affiliate

Washington, D.C.

Acts 10:34, 37–43; Psalm 118:1–2, 16–17, 22–23; Colossians 3:1–4, or First Corinthians 5:6–8; John 20:1–9

This is the day the Lord has made; let us rejoice and be glad in it.
—Psalm 118:24

Let us rejoice and be glad!

During the last few heavy days, as we accompanied Jesus' torture and death, we have had much to ponder: seemingly unending violence, climate change and impending ecological disaster, extremes of poverty and wealth in our own country and around the world, all vie for attention. At the same time, courageous people work for peace in the midst of war; generosity and compassion mark uncounted gestures in response to natural disasters; valiant work for a new global economy emphasizes social justice and the common good.

Our interpretation of the sacred story we are retelling in these days has to be shaped by this reality. Our understanding of the death and the Resurrection of Jesus Christ has to make sense in this contemporary context. That is the vocation of discipleship.

Let us think for a few moments about power: the power of nature, the power of greed, the power of weapons, the power of organized people, the power of courage, the power of community, the power of nonviolence, the power of good over evil, the power of love, the power of the cross, the power of life over death. . . .

This is the day the Lord has made; let us rejoice and be glad in it!

This is the day when we see the power of life over death, of nonviolence over violence, of good over evil, of love.

This is the day when the keening of women as they bury their children bears fruit in peace, when dialogue and negotiations replace war, when a global nonviolent peace force is fully funded and begins to grow.

This is the day when the yearning of all people for dignity and voice and hope is realized, when humility and honesty define leadership.

This is the day when unselfish generosity repairs the pain of natural disasters, when refugees and immigrants are welcomed, when diversity is seen as a gift.

This is the day when the common good becomes more important than having more, when healing takes precedence over privilege, when security rests in community and the satisfaction of basic needs.

This is the day when relationships are made right in every direction, when humans learn to live with each other and with the earth, when the healing of the nations and of the earth begins.

An opinion piece in the *Washington Post* right after the horrific tsunami hit Japan in 2011 asked if this was our "Lisbon moment," referring to the devastating Lisbon earthquake of 1755 that spawned a deep rethinking of assumptions about God and the meaning of human life. Such a rethinking is clearly appropriate in these times as well.

Like Jesus' friends (except some of the women), we struggle to understand the meaning of his life, death, and Resurrection. He would send us with them back to Galilee to retell the story so we could open it up again in our own context and reality, but all the while knowing its end.

As Jesus moved toward Jerusalem, deliberately engaging the powers and principalities of first-century Palestine, he also was building the beloved community, shoring them up in spite of themselves to nurture the seeds of life and hope even after he was gone. Fear and hatred stalked him all the way until, finally, betrayal, abandonment, torture, death—evil—prevailed. But it did not have the last word.

Today, all we can do is to stand in awe before the fact of the Resurrection and the hope it carries. Tomorrow we have to keep on telling this story of hope to see how Jesus' friends and followers tried to live it out. Just as they struggled to understand what it meant that he overcame evil, that he shifted the axis on which the world known to them was spinning, that he pointed their lives in a radically different direction, so must we.

Second Sunday of Easter

Fr. Michael Briggs, MM

Peru

Acts 2:42–47; Psalm 118:2–4, 13–15, 22–24; First Peter 1:3–9;
John 20:19–31

*Blessed be the God and Father of our Lord Jesus Christ! By
his great mercy he has given us a new birth into a living hope
through the resurrection of Jesus Christ from the dead. . . .*
—First Peter 1:3

Today we continue our celebration of Easter. The readings
today talk about fear, mission, and our common brotherhood
and sisterhood.

The Gospel text opens today with the disciples behind
locked doors because of their fear. This text is set on the Sunday afternoon after Jesus' death on Good Friday. So the disciples have a lot to fear after seeing the injustice, violence, and
death that Jesus suffered. But suddenly their apprehension
turns to joy as the risen Jesus appears in their midst. In contrast with the whirlwind of turmoil of the last days, Jesus' first
words are of peace. Then without wasting much time Jesus
sends the disciples in mission. And the mission is the identical
task that Jesus had been living as sent by his Father and that
had carried him to his violent death. Jesus is now giving it over
to the disciples. He also breathes on them and bestows on
them the Holy Spirit. They will not be alone in carrying out
this task. The mission implies forgiving sins.

We can probably all sympathize with Thomas. He was not
there when Jesus appeared, he has not seen anything, and he
wants evidence. And Jesus provides him that proof and adds,

"Blessed are they who have not seen and yet have come to believe." And John comments that this is recorded so that we might come to believe and thus have life in Jesus' name.

In the first reading we hear a description of the first Christian community. Emphasis is put on the wonders that the apostles did, the prayer, the breaking of the bread, and that those who believed shared all things in common.

So we find Jesus' presence overcoming the fear of the disciples. Jesus breathes on them the Holy Spirit and sends them in mission. And we see the early community choosing to share everything in common.

Aware that we are also being sent into mission, I find myself reflecting that many people are in need. Some have lost their jobs or their houses or are affected in vital ways by the reduction of government services. In Japan the population continues to be affected by the 2011 earthquake, tidal wave, and radiation from the nuclear plant. In rural Peru, more than 50 percent live in poverty and have deficient health services and inadequate education. Recent immigrants to the United States find themselves unwelcome. The challenges of living our solidarity are all around us.

However, just as in the Gospel of today, there is always the risk to find ourselves behind locked doors in fear and mistrust of the other. And this can paralyze us, blind us to the situation of the other, divide us into "us" and "them," and keep us on the sidelines.

I think the readings speak to these challenges. Christ is risen and Christ is here. We need not put our hope in keeping the door locked but rather celebrate that Christ is present. And Christ continues to send us in mission—the same mission that Jesus lived. And just as the first disciples had the intuition to put everything in common, maybe we are also called to be aware of all who continue to live in need, those who are excluded and marginalized. This implies opening the door, engaging in dialogue, building trust, addressing the issues of justice not only in our neighborhood but on a global scale.

In this time of Easter, as Jesus called forth Thomas to examine his wounds so that he might believe, Jesus is calling us to continue to examine his wounds today and believe in a more proactive way so as to continue his mission in the world.

Third Sunday of Easter

Sr. Genie Natividad, MM

Tanzania

Acts 2:14, 22–28; Psalm 16:1–2, 5, 7–10, 11; First Peter 1:17–21; Luke 24:13–35

Were not our hearts burning within us while he was talking to us on the road, while he was opening the scriptures to us?
—Luke 24:32

This third Sunday of Easter, we hear about the story of the two disciples leaving Jerusalem to go to a nearby village called Emmaus. As they were walking, Jesus came into their midst and walked with them on the road, but they did not recognize him. As I reflect on this Gospel, I ask myself, where in our day-to-day life do we find ourselves on the road to Emmaus?

The road indeed symbolizes the journey in Jesus' life. It was on the many roads he walked that he carried out his different ministries. Having this in mind, I ask myself, how often do I recognize Jesus walking with me on the road of life? This thought invites me to be more mindful of all the tiny events happening around me at each moment. It draws me to go deeper as I explore the culture of the people with whom I am called to walk. The road to Emmaus then is every road, every path we tread as pilgrims on this earth.

In Tanzania for several years now, I have been involved in a ministry called Watoto wa Vipapa (Children of the Pope). I work with children in a slum-like area. Five times a week I go to the parish to help the children with their lessons, and then I give them a religion class. Forty to fifty kids or more, of different ages and levels, come every afternoon for tutorials after their formal classes in different schools.

One time, a large number of our children, ninety-two of them, ages six to twelve years old, visited an orphanage and home for the elderly in another village about a thirty-minute drive from the parish. I took a dozen of the younger children in our car, and the others were packed in the bus. In spite of their being crammed in the vehicle, I sensed great excitement from them; they had prepared songs and dances, and some sweets and biscuits for the orphans. Many of the parishioners had responded generously and had given away used clothes, soap, and some cash for the orphans and the elderly.

Throughout our journey, I was deeply struck by the joyful and loud singing of the kids in the bus and our own car. They did not seem to mind being jammed into the vehicles. When we reached the orphanage, the children just filled the place and were so energized to mingle with the orphans. Some of them shared sweets and biscuits with them. As we waited for the younger orphans, we organized the kids in two lines and we started our long procession to the place where the elderly stayed, about a ten-minute walk. Upon reaching the place, they presented their song and dance to the elderly men and women. After their presentation, each of the children shook the hands of the elders as a sign of respect.

As we started our way back to the orphanage, the rain poured down. Many of us walked quickly, while the bigger kids started to run, all trying to reach the orphanage to take refuge from the rain. When we reached the orphanage, some of the younger children I was accompanying and I were quite wet. After few minutes the rain stopped, and the kids were able to sing and dance for the orphans. Our visit lasted for almost three hours. When I asked how the kids felt about their experience, they said they were happy, rather than complaining of hunger and overtiredness after all the travel, the walking and running, dancing and singing they had done. When we arrived back at the parish, the children's enthusiasm to go back to their homes to share the good news with their loved ones and friends was like a fire burning in their hearts.

Pope Benedict XVI said the road to Emmaus "is the path of renewal and maturation in faith for all Christians."

As I move to the heart of that experience, before leaving I felt challenged. It was a big job for me to handle such a big crowd of children of diverse ages, but it was full of fun and learning. It made me aware that on the road, the children encountered hardship, but their hearts were aflame as they met strangers on the road and joyfully welcomed them into their lives. As they continued walking, these children found new energy in their encounters with the orphans and the elderly. I sense the wonder of spiritual growth and appreciate the depths of faith in these young people. As a stranger entering deeper into the culture of this land, I can feel the hand of God leading me on the road and opening my eyes to see the wonder of the moment. Like the two disciples on the road to Emmaus, it is only in the journey that these children and I continued to encounter Jesus in those companions on the road who continually rekindled the fire of faith in our hearts.

Empowered by this Emmaus experience, I hope that these young people who teach me about life and who proclaim "Sisi ni wamisionari" ("We are missionaries") continue to grow in love of the Gospel—in caring and in solidarity with those who suffer. May they, like the disciples on the road to Emmaus, continue to discover a new sign of Jesus' presence wherever they are. May their encounters with the broken and glorious body of Jesus in their many journeys to Emmaus help them mature in faith and share the good news of Easter with hearts full of joy.

May each of us all be blessed with renewed hope as we walk on the road of life, savoring the many blessings of our journey, gifted with the eyes of faith that our risen Jesus walks with us, always present in the faces of those who surround us. Happy Easter to all!

Fourth Sunday of Easter

Fr. James H. Kroeger, MM

Philippines

Acts 2:14, 36–41; Psalm 23; First Peter 2:20–25; John 10:1–10

He calls his own sheep by name and leads them out.

—John 10:3b

"Shepherd me, O God, beyond my wants, beyond my fears, from death into life" is the refrain from a popular liturgical song by Marty Haugen; it is frequently heard at masses as the refrain of the responsorial psalm. It reflects the theme of today's readings. In fact, today is called Good Shepherd Sunday.

Now allow your imagination to move from today back to the 60s (not the 1960s) and travel to Rome. Many people were becoming Christians, and their faith was being severely tested. Both Saints Peter and Paul had been martyred between 64 and 67 under the persecution of Emperor Nero. Christians were being thrown to the lions in the Coliseum. (To commemorate their sacrifice the pope makes the way of the cross in the Coliseum on Good Friday.) In short, being a Christian demanded deep faith, even to the point of death.

One response of the Christians was to literally go underground; they met in the catacombs both to worship and bury their dead. What paintings did these early Christians place on the catacomb walls? The earliest and most frequent image was that of the Good Shepherd. Even in the most difficult of times, Christians felt Jesus' closeness to them. Even if they walked in the valley of the shadow of death, they trusted in Jesus' compassionate presence.

Through the centuries two images of Jesus as the Good Shepherd have been popular. One depiction has the shepherd carrying a lamb on his shoulders; another shows the shepherd in the midst of the flock guiding the sheep. Both images manifest the tender love of Jesus for the sheep, for you.

Quite naturally we can say, along with the early Christians, "The Lord is my shepherd, I shall not want. . . . He leads me. . . . I fear no evil." We hear Jesus' words spoken to us: "I am the good shepherd. The good shepherd lays down his life for the sheep. . . . I know my own and my own know me" (John 10:11, 14). Our faith is indeed a great source of consolation.

Frequently, when we think of shepherds in the church, we naturally, and correctly, think of the guiding role of the bishops, religious, and priests. However, the task can also be very validly applied to the pivotal role that others play in the Christian community, e.g., parents in the family, workers in a NGO seeking to protect migrants' rights, marriage counselors assisting struggling couples. Friends, along with the help of Jesus, you are to be a true shepherd for needy persons. Shepherding (it takes many forms) is your pathway to holiness. What is asked of you?

First, the true shepherd recognizes the needs of the sheep. Each person is unique, having a special personality and special needs. The sensitive shepherd is attentive and responsive to these very personal needs.

Second, the good shepherd is able to gather and guide the flock. In the family and society, ways of fostering unity and mutual compassion are important. Common activities, such as support groups, meals, even prayer, are essential.

Third, the shepherd is able to demonstrate caring and compassion, because he knows the weaknesses of the sheep.

Shepherds need to know when to apply tough love and when to forgive and overlook normal human failings. As coshepherds we readily turn to Christ the Shepherd and seek his guidance.

Last, shepherding demands feeding the sheep. Every person needs food for the body, the mind, and the soul. Genuine pastoral care requires looking after the physical, intellectual, and the crucial emotional-spiritual needs of people so they do not become "sheep without a shepherd."

These same guidelines readily apply to many persons in the Christian community; I think particularly of teachers and parish youth leaders. We all have the obligation to lovingly, and sometimes firmly, deal with others in a manner that reflects the sensitive compassion of Jesus.

On this Good Shepherd Sunday I choose to end this reflection on a very practical note by offering two concrete suggestions. First, you may wish to consider having two images of Christ present in the home. Of course, the crucifix is essential. You may also wish to purchase a picture of Christ the Good Shepherd with the sheep on his shoulder; it will serve as a reminder to imitate Christ, the chief shepherd Christ, in your ministry.

Finally, give yourself a special treat. Listen to the beautiful song "Shepherd Me, O God" by Marty Haugen. It is available free on a MP3 stream; simply Google "Haugen shepherd." Indeed, it will lead you—and those you shepherd—beyond your wants and fears into a deep contemplation of the Good Shepherd.

Fifth Sunday of Easter

Sr. Ann Hayden, MM

Nicaragua

Acts 6:1–7; Psalm 33:1–2, 4–5, 18–19; First Peter 2:4–9;
John 14:1–12

What they said pleased the whole community.   *—Acts 6:5*

Today's Gospel begins with "Do not let your hearts be troubled." And we can hear Jesus complete that thought saying, "Believe in God, and believe in me." We also know that we can trust Jesus' Spirit in us as well.

In 1986, when I arrived amid the contra war in Nicaragua, there was a shortage of almost everything except food, and it was rationed. Did people complain? Yes. Were the ordinary folk worried or anxious about the shortages of concrete and other building materials, of automobile and other machine parts, of medical supplies and of variety in one's diet? Not really. Instead, "Don't worry, innovate!" was the mantra of sufficiency that I heard over and over again early in my years of life and ministry in Nicaragua. Poets at heart, Nicaraguans are also humorists and love to tell of their inventive efforts to have enough in a time of shortage.

They reused junked iron and used what grew around them, like bamboo and adobe bricks instead of steel and cement. They studied the wisdom of the elders and returned to growing and using herbal medicines. They made new mechanical parts out of old ones, suggesting they used shoestrings and gum at times, too. And they celebrated the 1,001 uses of corn, their most abundant crop, in tasty recipes for the family.

Other needs, such as community wells, schools, health clinics, and latrine programs, were likewise met in creative, practical, and communal efforts to foster the common good in this struggling, economically poor but hopeful society. Competition and private gain were not a part of the effort. It was a human experience like many around the world when people living in poverty unite together with those who offer a partnership of solidarity to create space and opportunities for the whole community to benefit and grow.

In today's reading from chapter six and throughout the Acts of the Apostles, fresh and creative experiments in sustainability and sufficiency were the norm. It was all about life and the common good of the whole community. Mistakes were made and were corrected by assuring the participation of more, not fewer, in both innovative choices and in the benefits of sufficiency. The wisdom and the solidarity of the group were sought in prayerful practical decisions that "pleased the whole community." This is the kind of community experience that we long for and can only build if we rely on the Spirit of Jesus working within us, creating together the space and opportunities for all to benefit.

The reading from First Peter tells the early Christians to put their trust in Christ as the cornerstone of their community. We are called to build community in selfless service for the common good and through consuming less so the needs of all can be met. This may seem a stumbling block to those who accumulate goods and resources for personal gain but, to us who proclaim the life, truth, and way of Christ, this service in solidarity for the sake of the whole is a sign of being the people of God.

In Nicaragua, the mantra of sufficiency was a mantra of hope. Hope was the one thing we all clung to in those days, and we laughed to one another saying that if we lost hope it would be like putting the last nail in the coffin. It was all about survival for the one and for the whole. It was about building a home big enough for a whole nation.

Jesus tells the disciples that, in spite of their protests otherwise, they know the way home. Jesus shows us that the way home, the way to wholeness, can only be created in relationships of solidarity. We are called to serve the mission of Jesus that all may have life and have it in abundance. We must care for the earth's resources with creativity, innovation, solidarity, and with compassion in the hope that we can build with the earth a healthy and happy home for all.

Sixth Sunday of Easter

Br. Mark Gruenke, MM

Brazil; Mozambique; Namibia

Acts 8:5–8, 14–17; Psalm 66:1–7, 16, 20; First Peter 3:15–18; John 14:15–21

I will not leave you orphaned. —*John 14:18*

What does Jesus mean by not leaving us orphaned? When I was a missionary in Mozambique people would approach me frequently begging for help. Very often they would state that I should help them because they were orphans. Even adults would use this argument. One time a man about forty years of age argued that I should help him just because he was an orphan. I couldn't help myself. I responded unsympathetically. I said that I too (at fifty-five) was an orphan!

He seemed to have been very confused by my response. You see, to him I was far from being an orphan. I was looking at things using a very limited understanding of what an orphan is. For me, to be an orphan means that both my parents had died. But for that forty-year-old man it had a different meaning. To him, it meant that he had no person of means to whom he could turn in his time of need. Perhaps his parents were still alive, but they were as poor as or poorer than he was. They could not help him financially. He was without someone to whom he could appeal for help in time of necessity. When I said to him that I was an orphan too, he knew that it couldn't be true. He knew that I had all sorts of resources and contacts and support in my life.

The impoverished farmers to whom I ministered years ago in Brazil convey this same idea through an expression of theirs.

They frequently comment upon how important it is for everyone to have a big tree to shelter under. What they mean by this is that every poor person needs a wealthier person to whom he or she can appeal for help in time of need.

During his dialogue at the Last Supper, Jesus promised to be a shade tree for his disciples. And he promises this to us today as well. We are certainly encouraged to bring to him all of our needs and concerns, whatever they might be. But in today's Gospel, the context in which Jesus was making his promise not to abandon the disciples was very special. It was the evening when his Passion was to begin. Jesus was making this promise in the face of terrifying persecution. And Jesus knew that just as he suffered from persecution, so, too, would his followers be persecuted. Jesus was promising not to abandon them throughout the trials that lay ahead.

There is a paradox here. The Advocate that Jesus promises to send to them, the Spirit of truth, was the source of inspiration in his own life that led to his persecution! Jesus offers to send a Spirit that, if his disciples fully embrace the gift, will also lead them into persecution. Jesus says that the world cannot accept the truth, just as it does not accept him. The Spirit that Jesus sends is both a challenge and a comfort for his disciples and for us today.

In Namibia where I am now doing ministry there are many AIDS orphans. Because of the debilitating poverty of the majority of families, an orphan in Namibia is defined as a child who has lost at least one parent (not necessarily both). This is so because the loss of one parent seriously compromises the physical well-being of the child in a country where most people are struggling simply to survive. The church has programs to help AIDS orphans. These programs are aimed at helping the child stay with his or her remaining parent or to stay with his or her grandparents or with other relatives. The church is not building orphanages. A child needs to grow within a family. In Africa the family is the shade tree under which the child can grow and find the support that he or she might need throughout childhood and even later in life as an adult.

Jesus realizes that his followers need support as well. Just as following Jesus leads to estrangement and rejection, paradoxically, it also leads one into community. In today's Gospel, when Jesus uses the word "you," he is not talking to an individual. He is talking to all of his disciples gathered together with him. Jesus' invitation is not to establish a "Jesus and me" relationship. Jesus is inviting us to be united to one another in him. Christianity is a "we in Jesus" relationship. It is a communal relationship, just as Jesus is in the Father and we are in Jesus and Jesus is in us.

Jesus invites us to become part of his community. When we do so, we are joining with others who follow him out of love, who keep his commandments: Love the Lord, your God, with your whole mind, heart, and soul, and love your neighbor as yourself. The community that we are invited to join is big; as big, as the whole world.

Feast of the Ascension

Kathy Dahl-Bredine, former Maryknoll lay missioner

Mexico

Acts 1:1–11; Psalm 47:2–3, 6–9; Ephesians 1:17–23;
Matthew 28:16–20

*Go therefore and make disciples of all nations, baptizing them
in the name of the Father and of the Son and of the Holy Spirit.*
                               —Matthew 28:19

Throughout this Easter season we have worshipped with
renewed faith, but how hard it is not to doubt in these times
in which we now find ourselves, when at times the earth itself
seems to be failing us. Tsunamis, earthquakes, tornadoes,
floods in proportions not seen before. . . .

Where life is still somewhat comfortable, climate change
may still seem remote. In our indigenous Mixtec village of San
Isidro, Oaxaca, in southern Mexico, it is very real. In recent
years, rains came late, so farmers couldn't plant on their normal schedule. Then when it did begin to rain, it came in del-
uges and would not stop, until the corn and beans couldn't
mature for lack of sun. Then came a devastating early frost,
and the still-tender crops froze and turned black, leaving the
whole community and all those around the area with no harvest at all. No one can remember such a disaster happening
before. Here, where the people eat what they grow, a lost harvest doesn't just mean lost revenue; it means no food. The
main crops of the *milpa*—the corn, beans, and squash—are
the staple foods of the local traditional diet.

What was the reaction of the villagers? Our neighbors, Juan
and Carmelina, like all the villagers, have no insurance policies,

no bank accounts, only, if they're lucky, a few goats and sheep. When a special need arises, one can perhaps sell a goat. At the village Mass on the recent feast of St. Isidore, the patron saint of farmers, the people offered prayers for a good harvest for this coming year, with the steadfast faith that God, through our *Madre Tierra* (Mother Earth), will provide for them. Juan said hopefully, "This year will be better."

Jesus in his Ascension told us to go and spread the Word, make disciples—that is, to usher in the Reign of God, to observe what he had commanded us, and to remember that he is with us to the end of the world. In this Easter season we recall his last great commandment on Holy Thursday was that we love one another as he has loved us: the essence of the Reign of God. This love in action in today's world has to include sharing the resources of the earth that God has provided for all and respecting the other beings on this planet. Where can we find this Reign of God on earth today?

The people of San Isidro have that kind of faith. They know they depend directly on God's providence, and on Madre Tierra for life itself, and for the food and water to sustain life. Recently a new water project was initiated in the village, which for the first time ever brought piped water to every house in the village, instead of what has always been the custom: each villager having to laboriously carry one jug of water at a time on their donkey from the spring to their home, a considerable distance in many cases. On the day the water pump was to be first tested, the people gathered at a spot just above the spring on the mountainside, bringing traditional foods and drinks. First they dug out a little cave-like hole in the side of the mountain. Then, beginning with the eldest person in the village, each person present had to offer a small amount of each of the foods and a few drops of the drinks, into the hole, to request pardon of Madre Tierra for disturbing her and for the ways we have not properly respected the earth. At the same time as asking permission to begin this new project, they offered prayers to God for a blessing and for its success.

Where can we find the faith of those who are living the Reign of God? A friend of ours recently told us that when he was visiting, he realized he had more clothes than he needed. So he tried to give one of his good shirts to a local man. The man thought for a moment, then said, "No thanks, I have two shirts, so I don't need another one." Where do we find the Reign of God?

What is the cause of global warming? What is the cause of toxic oceans, dwindling fish populations, and polluted rivers? Here, where deforestation and eroded soils have been a challenge, people understand. They say, "We have not respected Madre Tierra as we should. It is our greed to have more, instead of just what we need to live." Can we look at our industrialized societies of the North and see the problem? Do we see that we, in our drive to be first in the world, to have more than everyone else, to create corporations that control the world, have continued taking more and more of the planet's limited resources in order to create wealth and power to control the world?

The economist David Korten says that on a scale of one to thirty-two in terms of resource use, we North Americans would be thirty-twos, while people living in rural areas in countries of the global South would be ones. In other words, each of us on the average is using thirty-two times the amount of water and other natural resources as a rural resident of southern Oaxaca. Can we learn a lesson from the people of San Isidro, their faith in God, and their willingness to live simply and depend on God's providence?

Pentecost Sunday

Kathy McNeely, former Maryknoll lay missioner

Guatemala; Maryknoll Office for Global Concerns

Acts 2:1–11; Psalm 104:1, 24, 29–31, 34; First Corinthians
12:3–7, 12–13; John 20:19–23

*For in the one Spirit we were all baptized into one body— Jews
or Greeks, slaves or free— and we were all made to drink of one
Spirit.* —First Corinthians 12:13

When I arrived in Nimlaha, an isolated village about seventy-
five kilometers and an entire day's journey from San Luis, the
municipality in Petén, Guatemala, where I was stationed as
a lay missioner, I stuck out: At five feet four, I towered over
the women and men who helped me carry my backpack to
the chapel where I would be talking with the women about
an upcoming leadership workshop. My translator, José Luis,
a native of San Luis, Petén, fluent in Spanish and in Qeq'chi',
was also new to Nimlaha, but one would never know. He was
greeted as an insider and conversed quite easily with everyone
we met.

We asked the women to assemble while we were offered
something to drink. Once they all took their seats, I launched
right in to my spiel about how my colleague and I were going
to be offering a women's leadership workshop the following
month, and how we wanted as many women as possible to
attend. José Luis dutifully translated. After telling them the
benefits of the workshop for about fifteen minutes I paused to
ask if they had any questions.

José Luis called on one woman in the front row. She wanted
to know if I ate greens like she did; I said yes, I did. Another

woman's hand shot up and she asked if I ate beans; again, I said yes. Immediately there was a third question, did I drink cacao (an indigenous chocolate drink)? I must have looked confused as I patiently said yes, I liked cacao and drank it. Sensing my puzzlement, José Luis asked the women why so many questions about what I ate? The woman from the front row explained that she wondered if I ate something different than what they ate because my skin and hair were so light in comparison to theirs.

This experience was not uncommon. What was unusual was the fact that the women were asking me to my face (through a translator) rather than talking about me behind my back. Frequently when I went to a new village, children would find a way to sit close to me and to touch my skin, count the freckles on my arm or stroke my hair. After a while the novelty wore off and they saw me as they saw others who lived in the village. I ate and drank the same things they enjoyed; I bathed in the river and slept in a hammock, much like any of them would do. These people, like humans all over the world, were very good at distinguishing differences. It takes people everywhere a lot longer to note the ways that we are all the same, or the ways that we are all interconnected.

I imagine it was difficult for Jesus' followers just after Jesus' death. I am sure his followers were very aware of the ways in which they stuck out. In following Jesus they were changed, and I am quite certain that in the weeks following his death, Resurrection, and Ascension, they were very aware of how Jesus was different and how he taught them to act differently from others in their society and faith tradition. Still, they hoped and believed that the Holy Spirit Jesus promised would help them to live that difference without Jesus in their midst.

It must have been shocking for them to receive the gift of the Spirit only to discover not how different they were from others, but how unified they were with all of creation, and how they could relate to other people as if they had all come from the same culture and were speaking the same language.

Diversity is good and necessary. It is the ingredients of beauty and new and creative possibilities. While I did not enjoy feeling so different from the people I met in Guatemala, I knew that I learned a great deal from them as I was immersed in their culture and that my presence challenged them and helped them to see the world from a different perspective.

The diversity represented by my presence planted seeds. The fact that I was one of a handful of single women on the parish team that visited villages and offered classes for women inspired a number of women to want to learn how to read and write. They decided that they wanted a woman to teach them, and they became motivated to send a few of their daughters to the city for high school education rather than arranging a marriage for them at the age of fourteen.

Today we celebrate this diversity but, more importantly, the gift of unity that is the Spirit of God. At Pentecost, Jesus' followers were filled with divine inspiration. Race, experience, social status, and language were no longer barriers as they "were all baptized into one body." Though they brought a diversity of gifts, they were united by being in one Spirit.

Let us pray on this feast of Pentecost that the gifts of the Spirit continue to embrace the global community, allowing us to cherish the differences and diversity while holding close to our hearts the ways that we are alike and interdependent on one another.

Holy Trinity Sunday

Fr. Raymond Finch, MM

Bolivia

Exodus 34:4–6, 8–9; Daniel 3:52–56; Second Corinthians 13:11–13; John 3:16–18

Indeed, God did not send the Son into the world to condemn the world, but in order that the world might be saved through him.
—John 3:17

Scientists tell us that the universe is expanding, growing. It cannot be contained. They tell us that everything is interconnected in ways that are so clear and complicated that we can only gaze in awe at the mystery of life that overwhelms, engulfs, and nourishes each one of us. It is revealing and amazing that the very complex compounds that are the building blocks of life were produced in the interior of stars that exploded billions of years ago. We are literally made of stardust. The universe, all life, all of creation is intimately interconnected and interdependent.

Today, we celebrate the Feast of the Holy Trinity: one God, three divine persons. Unity, built of diversity. Our faith tells us that the creation of the universe is the reflection of the Creator, that God is revealed in the complexity, interconnectedness, interdependence, simplicity, and unity of all creation. The Holy Trinity, God is reflected in creation, in the moments when we are aware of being one with the universe and during those moments when we see ourselves in the eyes of our brother or sister, moments of connectedness, moments being one in our diversity and moments when our strongest differences are simply a sign of God's creative power.

During my years as a missioner in Peru and Bolivia I have been privileged to live among people of many different cultures. I have lived in rural settings and in megacities; I have lived among the economically poor and among those who are better off. I have lived among subsistence farmers, factory workers, and university professors. I have lived among people of faith and people who are desperately searching, reaching out for something to fill the void. Many times I have been overwhelmed by what seemed to be profound differences. Yet, all in all, we are not as different as we might think. If we look each other in the eye, deeply, steadily we can see a bit of ourselves in each other. We can detect the stardust that is at the core of our being, the spark of divinity infused from the beginning in each of us.

Just as we can see the Holy Trinity reflected in the interconnectedness and interdependence of all creation, we also see the absence of God, sin, reflected in the divisions and walls that we build, in the differences that we exaggerate and use against each other. Each time that we abuse creation or each other, we injure ourselves and weaken the connectedness of all life that is revealed so clearly in the Holy Trinity. Each time that we rail against the profuse diversity that God continues to create, we turn our back on God and we cut ourselves off from each other and from the source of life.

The doctrine and image of the Holy Trinity manifests the force of love that cannot be contained, even within God, but flows out in the Son and Holy Spirit and through all of creation. We are called to oneness with that force of love, to go beyond ourselves and deepen our connectedness with one another and with the cosmos. Allowing ourselves to be gripped by the love manifested in the Holy Trinity is not simply an ideal, not simply a pious thought. It has clear and serious implications for how we live each day as well as for the structures and institutions that we have a part in creating and maintaining. We have a choice. We can build connections and grow in God's mission of love that overflows from the Holy Trinity, or we can build up walls and cut ourselves off from each other and our God. We can care for the parts of creation that have been entrusted to us, or we can abuse and deface creation for our own egotistical purposes. We can work for unity in our diversity, or we can retreat into a deadening uniformity. As we meditate on the Holy Trinity we are called to welcome the other, the stranger, and to see our reflection in their being. We are called to be inclusive, to invite others in rather than shut them out. We are called to care for creation rather than dominate it. We are called to live in the force of the divine love that constantly flows forth from the Holy Trinity and is the very source of our being and life. If we could only recognize and live this call, the world would truly be a different place.

Feast of Corpus Christi

Fr. Charlie Dittmeier, MM

Cambodia

Deuteronomy 8:2–3; 14–16; Psalm 147:12–15, 19–20;
First Corinthians 10:16–17; John 6:51–58

*Because there is one bread, we who are many are one body, for
we all partake of the one bread.* —*First Corinthians 10:17*

One of my earliest recollections of life in Asia was visiting the family of a poor, deaf student in a remote area in India. As smiling parents greeted us at the door of a small ramshackle house, I noticed a small boy go running out a back entrance with a handful of rupees. About ten minutes later he reappeared with a flapping, squawking chicken destined to be a special dish for the visiting guests. The poor family may have gone without food the next day in order to receive us properly.

Eating together is a significant human activity. Whether it's choosing who sits at "our" table in the school cafeteria or celebrating the Lunar New Year with an extended family cramped into a small Hong Kong flat, there are special dynamics at play. Along with the food, we share our stories and our lives; bonds are strengthened and renewed; new life and possibilities are created.

Jesus understood about eating. So much of his teaching and ministry is connected with sharing food with people he wanted to draw close to him. He spoke to them, listened to them, and shared all their experiences of daily life. But Jesus offered something more, not just an appreciation of the other or a happy memory after the meal was finished and people were walking home. He gave himself for the people to keep, for them to take home, for them to make part of themselves.

Three times Jesus said, "I am the living bread." It is a significant phrase for him. But what does it mean to be "living bread?" What does Jesus mean when he says, "Those who eat my flesh and drink my blood have eternal life?" It was not cannibalism, totally abhorrent to the Jewish people as it is to us. Rather, to consume Jesus means to assimilate totally into our being all that he teaches, his vision, his values, his understanding of the meaning and purpose of life. It means to be able to say with Paul in Galatians, "It is no longer I who live, but it is Christ who lives in me." His thinking is our thinking, his dreams are our dreams. The basic meaning of eating the body and blood of Christ is total union with him in the ways that we think and live.

Jesus needed people like him, people who thought and acted as he did, because he was soon to return to his Father and he wanted his work to continue. He was gathering, forming people to carry on God's work. Jesus probably did not intend to found a church such as we have today. Instead Jesus wanted a family of believers who could work together and support and strengthen one another to face the rigors and the dangers that he himself would face.

These were the disciples we read about in the Acts of the Apostles after Easter who went out from Jerusalem to invite and bring together rich and poor, slaves and free people, Jews and Gentiles, men and women. They came from different backgrounds and different experiences, but together they became God's family, brothers and sisters, and together they could overcome divisions and mistrust and enmity and find a new security, peace, and joy in life.

We are the disciples today, fed by the same body and blood of Christ, formed also into his body, and sent to invite and welcome others who do not yet know him. It is extremely important that we do so. Our world is even more divided than the world of Jesus and his disciples, but at the same time it is increasingly interdependent.

An earthquake and tsunami in Japan closes factories in Canada and Europe. Political upheaval in North Africa forces rethinking of strategic alliances in the capitals of the Western world. Migration from undeveloped countries because of persecution, economic conditions, or warfare unsettles traditional societies on other continents.

Increasingly we are challenged by events half a world away, and increasingly we must work out new ways of sharing our water, our air, our resources, our earth.

How do we do that? We celebrate and consume the body and blood of Christ, we take into ourselves his own self, and we become Jesus for the world. And then we open our minds, our hearts, our schools, our communities, our nations to all those God calls the children of God.

Is it easy? No. Is it necessary? Yes. It is God's will that we recognize that we are all God's children and that we must share our world and its resources, that we must seek what unites rather than what divides, that we overcome the prejudices that oppress and destroy. Only in this way will we find true peace within our own countries and within our one world.

Abraham Lincoln observed that "the best way to destroy an enemy is to make him a friend." If we eat the body and blood of Christ, if we truly become that which we eat, then we can have the eyes, the ears, the heart to form one family with all God's children.

Saints Peter and Paul, Apostles

Fr. Edward M. Dougherty, MM, Superior General,

Maryknoll Fathers and Brothers

Acts 12:1–11; Psalm 34:2–9; Second Timothy 4:6–8, 17–18; Matthew 16:13–19

But the Lord stood by me and gave me strength, so that through me the message might be fully proclaimed and all the Gentiles might hear it.   —Second Timothy 4:17

Every time our lives reach a significant new milestone, we join with family and friends in a joyous celebration. The same often occurs when we commemorate an anniversary at an organization that has become an integral part of our personal or work lives, and especially at one that deeply touches our hearts and souls.

For me and for those with whom I serve, along with the U.S. Catholic Church and sixty million Catholics across the country, 2011 marked a celebratory milestone within our church, commemorating a hundred years of mission.

Through our baptism, we all have been called to mission. During every day of our lives, we each have the opportunity to choose the way we wish to serve. Some people focus on prayer while others support their local communities. Some people provide donations to help the poor and disenfranchised, and some of us have been called to spread God's Word by living with and serving his flock around the world.

Our mission on behalf of the U.S. church began on June 29, 1911, our Foundation Day and the feast of Saints Peter and Paul. On this feast day, over a hundred years ago, Pope Pius X met with Father James A. Walsh of Massachusetts and Father Thomas F. Price of North Carolina, and he offered his blessing to the Catholic Foreign Mission Society of America. You know us as the Maryknoll Fathers and Brothers. One year later, Sister Mary Joseph Rogers began the Maryknoll Sisters. Along the way, our mission family within the U.S. church has grown to include the Maryknoll lay missioners and the Maryknoll Affiliates.

On this feast day, Catholics around the world recall Paul's conversion when Jesus identifies Paul as "an instrument . . . chosen to bring [his] name before Gentiles and kings and before the people of Israel" (Acts 9:15), and that Jesus blessed Peter for recognizing God's revelation and entrusted him with the mission of building God's Reign on earth. Collectively, all of us at Maryknoll work to keep the flame of mission burning brightly in the hearts of all U.S. Catholics.

Our centennial message, "The Gift of Mission—The Maryknoll Journey," commemorates a century of sharing God's love through the celebration of the Eucharist and the sacraments, the teaching of the faith, combating poverty, providing health care, building communities, and promoting human rights. We also marked this milestone by looking forward and finding new ways to continue our journey to provide religious education, offer academic and vocational training, foster sustainable agriculture and economic development, and encourage youth formation and interfaith dialogue.

Maryknoll currently is engaged in building God's Reign on earth through mission programs in twenty-eight countries that include the United States. In embracing the gift of mission, Maryknollers continue to share the Gospel and serve the poor in Asia, Latin America, and Africa while working to help animate U.S. Catholics to their baptismal call to mission.

During our first century, the more than two thousand Maryknoll Fathers and Brothers who have served in mission from parishes across the country have touched the lives of hundreds of thousands of people around the world. Our response to the mandate to spread the Gospel evolved as global human needs were encountered in the field afar, and caring for people holistically became our focus. We live among the people we serve. We enrich them and become enriched by them in return.

Our significant accomplishments, with the support of our bishops, parishes, and Catholics here at home, have included building the local church in all the areas we have served along with encouraging education and formation of local priests, brothers, sisters, and laity. During our history, Maryknoll also contributed to the peaceful transition of Japanese refugees out of China and back to postwar Japan during the 1940s, facilitated relief work in postwar Korea during the 1950s, provided medical care for AIDS patients in Africa, guided the poor who suffered during brutal regimes in Latin America, and ministered to those affected by the events of 9/11.

Today, as Maryknoll continues its mission journey into a new century with more than a hundred apostolic projects, we are recommitting ourselves to forge a Society that continues to be worthy of the sacrifices made by Maryknoll missioners during the first hundred years.

May all of us at Maryknoll continue to be stirred by a deep love of God, just as God's own love gives ultimate meaning to our lives. May we continue to be stirred by a deep love of Christ, the one who embodies the divine presence and reveals the face of God to us.

We are full of thanksgiving to Almighty God for the many blessings afforded us over this first century, and we pray that God will continue to bless each and every Maryknoller here at home and overseas—every Maryknoll Father and Brother and all of our Maryknoll Sisters, Maryknoll Associates, lay missioners and Maryknoll Affiliates, and all the people who partner with us in mission.

We seek the continued prayers and support of all members of the U.S. church to help us continue our mission journey to do God's work for another century. We also ask that all U.S. Catholics celebrate the gift of mission with us by renewing their baptismal call to mission.

Fourteenth Sunday in Ordinary Time

Sr. Cathy Encarnacion, MM

Philippines

Zechariah 9:9–10; Psalm 145:1–2, 8–9, 10–11, 13–14;
Romans 8:9, 11–13; Matthew 11:25–30

But if Christ is in you, though the body is dead because of sin,
the Spirit is life because of righteousness.   *—Romans 8:10*

"You ask us if we own the land. And mock us, 'Where is your title?' Such arrogance of owning the land when you shall be owned by it. How can you own that which will outlive you?" So asked Macliing Dulag, a tribal chieftain hero who led the opposition against the establishment of the Chico River Dam in the Cordilleras, Philippines, a project conceived without the knowledge of the affected indigenous peoples. He was killed by the military during the Marcos era.

In this quote Macliing Dulag speaks to the reverential attitude evoked in each person in the presence of the great beauty and grandeur of creation. Certainly this Sunday's readings elucidate for us that such an attitude is natural, for God is the king of all creation and for all times. Zechariah tells us that God is king, not to demand domination and control but to present peace, entering into the city atop a donkey and not a war horse. If God in God's greatness can come to us as gently as one riding a donkey (in Jewish tradition symbolizing a friendly and solemn entry) and not aggressively as one going to war, could we do otherwise?

Living and working now in the northern part of the Philippines, known in my childhood for its cool weather, fresh clean air, and hills peppered with the pine trees, I cannot but lament now the brown-barren mountains, the smog-laden air, and subdivisions daring to name themselves after breathtaking vistas that are now sorely missing. Since I have integrated the deep-rootedness and sensitivity to the land that the indigenous peoples teach, I feel quite sad and disappointed that this area, third largest in terms of populations of tribal peoples in the Philippines, could come to this sorry state. Have they, like most of us educated in the modern ways and Western orientation, slowly drifted away from their oneness with the land? Are they losing their pulse for other created beings? Or has the lure of development and progress given them reasons to let go of the long-held values of oneness, communion, and integration in exchange for long-term familial security?

Fortunately, in the reading from the Letter to the Romans, there is the assurance that although we as persons from all races and traditions may deviate from our identity as persons in whom the same spirit that raised Jesus Christ from the dead dwells, we are always invited to turn our backs on that which separates us from God and walk with the Spirit. Undoubtedly, when making everyday decisions with limited resources in order to raise a healthy family in safe and well-off surroundings, we will make concessions. The big struggle is what to give up and what to hold on to. Could a mother decide to hold on to family heirlooms like headdresses inherited from generations of foremothers, to preserve a concrete part of their heritage if it means seeing her children go hungry? Or could a father decide not to cut down old hardwood trees in order to protect the forest and all life-forms depending on it when it means that his family may not have decent shelter? Happily, the choices we are asked to make are not always so difficult, and careful consideration and wholesome actions respectful of many more sensibilities of people and land can usually be taken.

A good example of this is one of our current projects to rebuild the huts in the village station of our Cosmic Journey here at the Maryknoll Sisters Center for Justice, Peace and Integrity of Creation, which were destroyed during Typhoon Juan in October 2010. Since we too work with limited monetary donations, we try to be very creative. After consulting with indigenous hut builders, the Department of Natural Resources and their foresters, staff, and frequent guests, we felt we were able to cut some of our older trees to rebuild the huts for which we have the funds, while leaving peacefully undisturbed the only century-old tree in existence here in Baguio City. We promised to plant even more trees this year than we did the previous years. And, before we proceeded to cut down the trees, we held a ritual to honor the spirits in the life of the trees. It was solemn, truly respectful of the indwelling of the Spirit in Creation and a profound recognition of God as the source of all. I was blissfully roused from my melancholy to feel and experience how deeply rooted still the indigenous people are in the land, and so was able to acclaim and exalt God, whose kingship and dominion is for all times and who constantly invites the weary and heavy-laden, for with God our yoke is easy and our burdens are made light.

Fifteenth Sunday in Ordinary Time

Barbara Fraser, former Maryknoll lay missioner

Peru

Isaiah 55:10–11; Psalm 65:10–14; Romans 8:18–23;
Matthew 13:1–23 or 13:1–9

For as the rain and the snow come down from heaven, and do not return there until they have watered the earth, making it bring forth and sprout, giving seed to the sower and bread to the eater, so shall my word be that goes out from my mouth.
— Isaiah 55:10–11

Although he was small, Leonel looked far more mature than his ten years when he climbed aboard the train high in the Andes of Peru. Polite and very serious, he sat down on one of the hard wooden benches and said he was going to visit his brother in Juliaca, a city about half an hour away.

Like most Andean people, Leonel was from a farming family. He had the dark skin and high cheekbones of the Quechua Indians who were his ancestors, and like them, his family lived close to the land, mainly growing potatoes. Could they make a living at that? He shrugged. It depends on the weather, he said. If there's a good harvest, yes; if the harvest is bad, we don't have enough to eat. We go hungry.

The train rumbled past fields where crops flourished, like the description in today's psalm—the furrows had been watered; the hills seemed to overflow with abundance. But Leonel's family and millions of other people around the world who depend on tiny plots of land for their livelihood know they are at the mercy of the weather.

A good harvest means they will have enough to eat, with a little left over to sell at the market to buy shoes, notebooks, and pencils so their children can go to school. A late frost, drought, or too much rain can mean a poor harvest or none at all. That brings hunger and forces family members, or the entire family, to move to the city in search of work.

Every spring, throughout the Andes, farmers plow their fields with oxen, if they can afford it, or make rows with a hoe. Usually the man opens the furrow and the woman drops in the seeds, covering them carefully. How much promise, how much hope is contained in a tiny seed! And how much the farmers depend on the weather, or the price of seed or transportation, factors largely beyond their control.

Today's readings are filled with images of planting and growing, images familiar to the people of Old and New Testament times, who, like Leonel's family, depended on the land for their livelihood. They knew that a farmer sows seeds without knowing what the future will bring.

Nowadays, farmers must contend with forces that were unimaginable just decades ago. In recent years, we have seen how a drought in Australia or an increase in oil prices in the Middle East can affect food prices everywhere in the world. If prices of seeds and supplies increase, families like Leonel's, who grow just enough for their own survival, can no longer make a living and must leave their farms or go hungry.

In Africa, governments of desert countries that do not have enough farmland of their own are buying large tracts of land in other countries to grow crops that they can import to feed their own people. They safeguard their own food supplies at the expense of small farmers in those other countries, who have less and less access to land.

For those of us who live in cities or suburbs and shop at grocery stores, it may be difficult to imagine the life of the family that plowed, planted, and cultivated the food we buy. But we are all part of an immense web of people, plants, animals, weather, and markets that spans the globe. Climate change, to which our actions contribute, especially affects poor farmers in Africa, Asia, and South America, who are faced with drier conditions, unseasonal weather, and unusually severe storms.

Even if we do not grow our own food, we can stand in solidarity with the people who grow crops to feed their families and ours.

In today's Gospel, Jesus compares the Word of God to the seeds scattered by the farmer. Sometimes we are fertile soil, letting God's Word take root in us. Sometimes we are rocky ground, where God's Word competes with weeds for our attention.

But it is not enough to simply listen to God's Word. We are called to be the fertile ground that allows the seed to grow and spread, that nurtures it and brings it to fruition. Isaiah speaks of this: "So shall my word be that goes forth from my mouth; it shall not return to me empty, but it shall accomplish that which I purpose, and succeed in the thing for which I sent it."

We must receive the Word of God, not as passive listeners, but as Christians committed to doing God's will. We are called to respond to those in need, to speak out against injustice, to care for God's creation—to spread the seed, God's Word, to others. When we act in justice and love—in our families, in our communities, and beyond—we ensure that God's Word does not fall on rocky ground, that it does not return empty, that it achieves God's purpose in our lives and in the world.

We are not alone in this task. Our Christian community strengthens us, calls us to faithfulness, helps us open our hearts to receive the seed that is God's Word and discern how God is calling us to act. In midsummer, as crops flourish in the fields, this is a fitting time to ask ourselves: How are we listening and responding to God's Word? What actions are we taking to respond to issues of economic injustice and climate change which disproportionately affect the poor? What are we doing to ensure that the seeds of justice, mercy, and solidarity bear a fruitful harvest in our parish or Christian community?

Sixteenth Sunday in Ordinary Time

Fr. Ken Thesing, MM

East Africa; Rome

Wisdom 12:13, 16–19; Psalm 86:5–6, 9–10, 15–16;
Romans 8:26–27; Matthew 13:24–43 or 13:24–30

The kingdom of heaven may be compared to someone who sowed good seed in his field.   —Matthew 13:24

In our scripture readings this morning we come up against the problem of evil. Just as we today struggle with this, asking, "Why do babies die, why do the innocent suffer, why doesn't God punish the evil ones?" so in past times, as the reading from the Book of Wisdom says, evil was a problem. And it says God uses God's power, not to punish but to save . . . and God wants us all to do the same today. That is a challenge!

In the Gospel Jesus uses a parable to communicate that we should learn to be patient, learn to live with difference, know the difference but not exclude or try to remove all differences from our life, from our communities, from our world. Jesus uses the example of wheat and weeds in a field. We might use examples such as people of different color, or religion, or culture, or economic status. Jesus says to be patient with these differences as he relates the parable of the wheat and the weeds. He warns us not to do something rash.

I remember an episode from thirty years ago. I came back to the United States from my mission in Tanzania, and I was visiting my brother and his family at their farm. As farmers always do, we went out to look at the fields and crops. My brother asked me, "Look, do you recognize these weeds?" I replied, "No, I don't think I have ever seen them before; how did they get into your fields?" He said, "Some years ago herbicides were developed; the weeds and grasses we struggled with in the crops when we were growing up have all been eliminated. All these seeds were just lying there dormant in the ground; they could not compete earlier with the dominant weeds and now they have sprouted and come forth."

We talked about this. My brother said farming is like life; there will always be challenges, always be differences. We need to be patient and tolerant, to recognize the problems, the evil amid the good, and find ways to work with it and around it.

I told of an experience I had had in Tanzania. We had a severe, long drought, followed by severe food shortage; people were hungry and could find nothing to eat. With gifts we had received from abroad we bought food and distributed it to those with nothing to eat. One day I got upset when I saw school teachers in line for food. I said, "Why are you in line? You have salaries, go and buy food; this is for those who have nothing." They looked at me and one teacher said quietly, "Yes, Father, but there is no food to buy. I walked ten miles yesterday to a village to buy food; there was none." He pointed to another teacher. "He went twenty miles on a bicycle to another place we heard there may be food. He found nothing. We and our families are hungry too."

I recognized that I, like the man in the parable, had weeds in my field of wheat. I was intolerant of others; I was judgmental. I was not recognizing the differences; I was trying to judge the good and the bad by my criteria. I was not patient.

One year in the parish where I worked, I started a small project with a group of young catechists. I helped them apply modern planting and weeding methods to a cotton field. There was a really good result, a large harvest. I was pleased, and so were they. The next year when I mentioned it was time to prepare and plant our field they were quiet and downcast;

they looked away. When I asked what was wrong they said, "Father, it's our families, our fathers, brothers, uncles who say, 'Oh, now you want to do like the *mzungu* (the foreigner); are our ways not good enough for you?'" The catechists said, "Father, be patient with us and with our families. There are so many things happening, so much change going on in our lives now. We need our families; they need us. We will change, and so will they but it will take time."

When I reflect on our scriptures this morning I see the wisdom in God's Word. Yes, God does have power, and so we do have grounds for hope. But God knows we are impatient; we are judgmental and often think what is different from us is evil and has to be uprooted now. But I think Jesus teaches us in the parable of the wheat and the weeds that the line separating good and evil is in our hearts, in the heart of every person. Evil is not outside us, between you and me or between individuals, one good, one bad; it is not between groups of individuals or between nations, exhibiting a need to immediately uproot the bad. No, evil is in the hearts of every one of us; there is good and evil in us all.

So I believe our lesson today is this: be calm, be patient and tolerant, and do not be judgmental. Know that even as there is evil present in the world, the power of God is present. So let us be people of hope. And then recognize the weeds in our own heart, the evil that still resides there with the good; know that the love of God will one day destroy it as God's love already has destroyed the power of evil in and through Jesus. For now, recognize the seeds of those weeds, work to keep them from sprouting, but be patient with yourself, with others and their differences. Try to understand them and appreciate them. Overcome evil with good, says Saint Paul in our second reading, from the Letter to the Romans. The Spirit of God prays for us too; this prayer will certainly be heard. Be hopeful.

Seventeenth Sunday in Ordinary Time

Kathy McNeely, former Maryknoll lay missioner

Guatemala; Maryknoll Office for Global Concerns

First Kings 3:5, 7–12; Psalm 119:57, 72, 76–77, 127–130;
Romans 8:28–30; Matthew 13:44–52 or 13:44–46

Give your servant therefore an understanding mind to govern your people, able to discern between good and evil.

— *First Kings 3:9*

If you were able to ask for anything knowing it would be granted, what would it be? Solomon found favor in God's eyes when he asked for, and was granted, wisdom. In these tough economic times, would wisdom be your request?

In the United States we are so used to a world where individual value is somewhat defined by how much money a person earns or what kind of "stuff" that person owns. But this world is foreign to what Jesus talked about as he discussed with his followers the kingdom of heaven—the new world that we as Christians are challenged to build on earth. The parables Jesus shares about God's Reign are an entry point to think more deeply about the choices we make in a society where stuff (and its acquisition) flourishes.

"The kingdom of heaven is like treasure hidden in a field, which someone found and hid; then in his joy he goes and sells all that he has and buys that field." It seems that in today's world, once the treasure is found, the right to mine what sits under the land (rather than the land itself) is bought or leased so that more extraction can happen. This passage calls to mind the Yellowstone River that flows through one of the United States' national treasures, Yellowstone National Park. In July

2011, the Silvertip pipeline released an estimated 42,000 gallons of crude oil into that river. This disaster, brought about by the ExxonMobil Pipeline Company, which operates Silvertip, stands as just one example of the countless places around the world where mining for resource like oil, gas, metals, and chemicals (to make the energy systems, gadgets, and gewgaws that define our way of life) are recklessly disrupting national treasures and people's livelihoods, and are polluting water systems.

Jesus continues, "The kingdom of heaven is like a merchant in search of fine pearls; on finding one pearl of great value, he went and sold all he had and bought it." The ethic of the mainstream economy would have the merchant buying the new pearl on credit so that he can hold on to the rest of his stuff for a while before having to sell anything. Oh, how difficult it is to part with our stuff. In a society defined by credit, we barely pay off one debt before we are in debt again.

Finally, Jesus teaches, "The kingdom of heaven is like a net that was thrown into the sea and caught fish of every kind; when it was full, they drew it ashore, sat down, and put the good into baskets but threw out the bad." I hardly think that Jesus' parable applies to today's fishing practices where bottom trawling (dragging giant weighted nets along the ocean floor) rips up and destroys ancient coral forests and other ocean life, where as many as four pounds of unwanted, undersized fish are thrown back dead or dying for every one pound of cod, rockfish, or shrimp that is brought to market.

For our modern-day urban-dwelling society, these parables may seem hard to understand. In the United States especially, people who live in cities are often unfamiliar with the extraction process that brings gasoline to fuel pumps or natural gas to stoves and hot-water heaters. Precious little thought goes into the source of the metals and minerals that make cell phones and laptop computers. We think little about using credit and accumulating stuff. It is not every day that the origin of food crosses our minds, nor whether it was produced or caught in a safe and sustainable manner.

As a lay missioner in Guatemala in the 1990s, I became aware of the deep understanding that the indigenous people with whom I worked had of these parables. Because their lives and livelihoods were so connected to the earth, they had an incredible awareness of even small changes in their ecological surroundings. National treasures, like the ancient Mayan ruins, were cherished with awe and reverence. Even the earth itself was honored before planting with a *Mayahak*, a ritual to feed the earth, offering it food, drink, and sweet-smelling incense to ask permission for breaking it open and sowing seeds. Mountains, rivers, and lakes were thought to have personalities, and they could get angry if humans overstepped their proper relationship with them.

This kind of wisdom is foreign to urban dwellers who are often in positions of power to make decisions about what kind of development is needed in isolated rural communities around the world. For many of these decision makers, progress would be the mechanization and urbanization of these rural areas. But in this process so much culture and wisdom of the natural world would is lost.

What a different world we would live in if we had Solomon's wisdom today, if we could really understand the parables as Jesus told them to simple people, in touch with the land and its treasures, in touch with finding and keeping real beauty rather than mindlessly accumulating stuff, and aware of how important it is to take just what is needed and to throw the rest back.

Let us pray today for the wisdom of Solomon, a wisdom that "brings out of his treasure what is new and what is old."

Eighteenth Sunday in Ordinary Time

Sr. Rose Gallagher, MM

Thailand

Isaiah 55:1–3; Psalm 145:8–9, 15–18; Romans 8:35, 37–39;
Matthew 14:13–21

*And all ate and were filled; and they took up what was left over
of the broken pieces, twelve baskets full.*   —*Matthew 14:20*

Today's readings are God's invitation to an ongoing banquet, offered out of a heart overflowing with unconditional love, for all peoples of whatever religious tradition. Isaiah voices God's promise of waters that will satisfy our thirsting hearts. The psalmist tells of the Lord's goodness and kindness offered to all. Paul exhorts us to have faith in the promise that despite the challenges of life, nothing will separate us from Christ's love. Matthew's Gospel prefigures the supreme and eternal gift of God's self to us in the Eucharist, when his compassionate heart satisfied a hungry population searching for his truth.

As we look around us we see a troubled world: chaos in the Middle East, people struggling for basic human rights, families divided in loyalties. Also, here in our own country, we share like disorders in relationships in our competitive society where wealth and position rule over a large majority of our people struggling to be accepted as persons of worth, despite their lack of economic status. Our world is hungry and thirsts for the peace that God holds out to all peoples and longs to be embraced by God's love, which alone brings comfort to troubled hearts. Is there a way this can be realized? The answer is "Yes." Pope John Paul II said, "God would like the history of humanity to be a fraternal journey in which we accompany one another toward the goal which [God] sets for us." One way we do this is through interreligious collaboration.

For many years, while working in Thailand, I was blessed to know and be assisted by an outstanding Buddhist follower named Lady Kanita. She received this title through her many decades of humanitarian services to her people. In my attempt to establish a safe shelter for women and children who had been violated in multiple ways, I sought her advice. Through her experiences of caring for those outcast by society, she knew best how to encourage me to show unwavering compassion, kindness, and understanding for all who would seek shelter and protection at our center. As I listened to this great woman with ears wide open I felt the God called by many names present to each of us.

Kanita's center, called the Promotion of the Status of Women, has sheltered thousands of victims who have been preyed upon by unscrupulous predators who roam through villages and communities seeking out those who are poor and vulnerable. Kanita was called upon often to speak to religious communities in Thailand about her work, its successes, and challenges; in turn, she expressed admiration and was inspired by the many outreach services offered by Catholic groups in which cooperation was a part of ongoing efforts together. At our Women's Desk and safe shelter for victims of multiple forms of violence, I tried, with the staff, to exhibit similar virtues when caring for all those who came in search of healing. Our programs focused on people's personal worth, confidence in the truth that through people's innate goodness, self-esteem could be restored and a belief that, and with a connected support system, rehabilitation assured a sense of wholeness that in turn benefited society at large.

The lessons learned from Lady Kanita and the testimony given by Bishop Michael Bunluen Mansap of Thailand speak volumes to all who seek true relationships with followers of other religious traditions: "Working with my Buddhist friends in the field of peace and justice, I feel inspired by their simplicity of life, their openness, their human relationships and their unassuming ways in dealing with others. This is the Good News that the Buddhist give us. They are evangelizing us."

Pope Paul VI saw dialogue as a new way of being church, not just with other religions, but with the world at large. God is in dialogue with people and religions; we must learn to listen to God speaking to people.

The deeper I am rooted in God, the more I can branch out in relationship to other religions, cooperating with, learning from, and by being enriched by the "other" who holds like truths of the One who is the Way, the Truth, and the Life of all.

Jesus' invitation is offered to all peoples: Are you thirsty? Come and drink from Jesus' source. Are you hungry? Eat abundantly from Jesus' table. Jesus' love is unconditional; all he asks is for your love in return. We ask ourselves today, "How am I responding to Jesus' invitation to drink and eat at this banquet of love? How do I collaborate with others whose religious beliefs differ from mine?"

Nineteenth Sunday in Ordinary Time

Kathleen Bond, Maryknoll lay missioner

Brazil

First Kings 19:9, 11–13; Psalm 85:9–14; Romans 9:1–5;
Matthew 14:22–33

Jesus immediately reached out his hand and caught him.
—Matthew 14:31

Matthew's words in today's Gospel invite me to reflect on how Jesus' hand continues to reach out and catch people who are afraid and struggling. In São Paulo, the fifth-largest city in the world, with an estimated population of twenty million, many people are immigrants either from other parts of Brazil or more recently from Bolivia and Africa. Despite Brazil's international image of an emerging economic powerhouse and host of the upcoming Olympics and World Cup, Brazil is a rich country with many poor people. Eight percent of the population subsists on less than $50 a month in the government-named economic class *miseráveis,* "the miserables ones." Unfortunately, the daily reality for recent arrivals is harsh as many face employment in sweatshop conditions, endemic urban violence, overcrowded public transportation, and poor public health and education services. Like the disciples in the Gospel, these folks are on a boat, and the conditions are pretty shaky.

I see Jesus' outstretched hands in the work of Welcome House, a transitional home for women run by the St. Vincent Pallotti Sisters in the center of São Paulo. The house provides food, shelter, and social services for thirty-five women refugees and former prisoners from other countries as they try to rebuild their lives. Previously, foreign prisoners often languished in jail here even after serving their sentences because they did not have a permanent address in Brazil. The Welcome House provides a safe place for those who work to earn money to buy a ticket back to their own country. For other refugees, who often are accompanied by their children, the Welcome House helps them establish their new life in Brazil.

One of the many women welcomed by the sisters is Rebecca. In 2009, Rebecca was on a shopping trip to Brazil for her business in Angola. On the plane over she met a woman, and they decided to share a hotel room. When the police raided their room, drugs were discovered, and Rebecca and the woman were arrested. According to Rebecca, she did not know that the other woman was in possession of drugs. After a short time in jail, Rebecca received an alternative sentence of community service. The judge did not specify a specific work site or a length of time. Rebecca lives in limbo with the constant possibility of returning to jail if her alternative sentence is revoked.

Rebecca and seven other women from Angola, the Congo, Greece, and South Africa participated in a course that I facilitated on women's health. Many of the women suffer from menstrual pain, fibroids, back problems, and stress. The course opened up a space for the women to share their stories, learn more about health issues, and seek solutions to their problems. In the process, many of the women reflected that participating in the group has helped them connect on a deeper level with each other at a moment of transition and tension. During the final evaluation, Rebecca related that the course helped her gain self-confidence. Even though she had lived in the house for over two years, she did not feel that she was close friends with any of the women. The course gave her an opportunity to open up and make friends. Rebecca found

the sessions on menstruation helpful because she often experiences debilitating monthly pain. She is trying to put into practice the exercises and diet modifications introduced during the
course. After many unsuccessful months of searching for a job,
she is excited to begin working as a seamstress.

Through the work of the Pallotti Sisters' Welcome House,
Jesus stretched out his hand and caught Rebecca, Augusta,
Cristina, Nifi, Melinda, Yolanda, Marcela, and many others. A
strong theme in Catholic social teaching is solidarity. We are
one human family independent of our nationality, religious
affiliation, or ethnic group. May we all heed the sisters' example of welcoming the stranger in our midst.

Feast of the Assumption (August 15)

Jason and Felicia Gehrig, former Maryknoll lay missioners

Bolivia

Revelation 11:19, 12:1–6, 10; Psalm 45:10–16;
First Corinthians 15:20–26; Luke 1:39–56

And why has this happened to me, that the mother of my Lord comes to me?   —*Luke 1:43*

Today we celebrate Mary, the mother of Jesus, who is so dear to people of faith throughout the world. This Jewish woman, revered by Christians, is also considered one of the most righteous in Islam. Our relationship with Mary is as diverse as it is profound, from my German-American grandmother who, up to the hour of her death, continued her lifelong devotion to Mary asking for her intercession; to our Aymara and Quechua neighbors of El Alto, Bolivia, who would solemnly join together on evenings leading up to Mary's feast day to chew coca leaves and light candles to venerate her.

In today's Gospel reading, we hear of our Savior's pregnant mother visiting her elder relative Elizabeth, herself also with child. Perhaps seeing the hand of God in Elizabeth's pregnancy as well as in her own, Mary sought her cousin's presence for mutual support and shared joy. Whether in times of recognition of the presence of the divine in our lives or in times of critical need, we seek community. Being in Maryknoll mission in an impoverished, semiurban neighborhood of the Bolivian Andes often allowed us to be present in the unfolding of moments strikingly similar to such biblical accounts. Recalling Mary's visit to Elizabeth brings to mind another encounter of much-needed spiritual support between two mothers.

Charo, our neighbor and mother of four grown sons, had made her way to the rented, adobe home of Magdalena, a young Aymara first-time mother of twin baby girls, one of whom had just died. Charo's consolation of Magdalena reflected the dire poverty they faced: "Perhaps it is best that God took your little one home. You have been suffering for six months with your infirm one. Now you'll have the strength and milk to be able to take care of your remaining child well." There in the one-room home's dirt floor lay Magdalena's lifeless little one, wrapped in a white cloth with a single light bulb lit above her body. The wooden fruit crate Charo had brought along with her was being crafted into a small casket by Magdalena's husband. As Charo prayed over the little child, she assured the young, questioning mother that her precious, unbaptized baby would most certainly be received by our loving God with open arms. A little broom, sandals, and angel wings were fashioned out of straw and placed in the casket to assist the little one on her journey home.

This modern-day visitation, occurring on a daily basis among too many of the world's impoverished mothers, points to some of the reasons why people of faith are drawn to Mary throughout the world. Knowing that Mary too was present at her son's execution—her enduring the agony of a parent seeing her beloved child taken from her—draws us to her in times of dire need and in time of mourning. And yet, her unique relationship as mother of Jesus, our Redeemer, and her faithful witness to his earthly ministry, culminating in his Resurrection, also draws us to her in a spirit of fortitude, hope, and renewal.

The humanity of God incarnate in the person of Jesus was most closely shaped by his mother Mary from his origins in her womb to her presence in his final days on earth. Undoubtedly, the suffering of Mary's community under the oppression of foreign rule and local, complicit leadership heightened Jesus' awareness of humanity's shortcomings as well as promise. Yet it was from these oppressive margins of Mary's time and place that God chose to bring clarity to all of creation through Jesus Christ, "God among us," and "the Son of Man, laying forth God's plan of love and reconciliation for each of us and our many diverse communities of faith and life.

To understand Mary, we must be able to see her face among today's marginalized masses of humanity crippled by the daily violence of poverty. Just as Mary's life took place in Judea under a Roman occupation utilizing local secular and religious leaders to keep the oppressed population in check, so too was the Bolivian society known by Charo and Magdalena through the early 2000s marked by a majority indigenous population systematically excluded from power.

Both then and now, these women struggle to attain a sense of hope and opportunity under a global power system that subjugates weaker societies, generating misery and resentment. The Canticle of Mary, or Magnificat, included in today's Gospel of Luke, reflects this sense that the powerful are brought down from their thrones and the lowly lifted up. It is not a call for vengeance, but rather an acknowledgement that even those considered of little worth in the eyes of the world are indeed considered fully dignified and beloved in the eyes of God. May we strive to see as God sees. May God's grace help us set aside our worldly ambitions so that we can see, and befriend, Mary among the marginalized masses of our own time.

On this feast day of the Assumption of Mary, we give thanks to God for the faithful inspiration she provides us to this day. We relish, and seek to emulate, Mary's openness to God's calling and faithfulness to Christ's mission. In doing so, may we lowly one day join Mary in also being called blessed.

Twentieth Sunday in Ordinary Time

Br. John Beeching, MM

Thailand

Isaiah 56:1, 6–7; Psalm 67:2–3, 5–6, 8; Romans 11:13–15, 29–32;
Matthew 15:21–28

Woman, great is your faith! Let it be done for you as you wish.
> —*Matthew 15:28*

I've always liked the story of the Canaanite woman in chapter 15 of Matthew's Gospel, for a couple of reasons. First, because I had a somewhat similar experience shortly after being assigned by Maryknoll to Thailand, and second, because it records an instance where Jesus is shown to be just as human as the rest of us—something we sometimes tend to overlook. He felt hunger, thirsted, cried, got angry, so much so that he flipped over tables, and he could be irritated and show impatience. He was after all, a human being. As such, he quite naturally shared the biases and prejudices of his own time and culture.

The story of the Canaanite woman, as Matthew recounts it, is about someone who couldn't take no for an answer, who simply wouldn't shut up, a woman so pushy that her pestering finally provoked a sharp remark from Jesus: "It is not fair to take the children's food and throw it to the dogs." How like the rest of us! When we are irritated or pushed to our limits, subliminal prejudices kick in, stereotypes, and we find ourselves saying something we later regret or feel ashamed about. The disciples are unable to get rid of the woman, and neither can Jesus, even with his remark about bread and dogs. The woman persists with a cunning play on words. "Yes, Lord," she responded, "yet even the dogs eat the crumbs that fall from their masters' table." Unexpectedly, Jesus not only answers her plea and heals her daughter but praises her faith: "Woman, great is your faith! Let it be done for you as you wish." Perhaps it is important to note that the only two people whose faith Jesus singles out for praise are not from among his own faith community. He praises the faith of a Canaanite woman and that of a Roman centurion— "I tell you, in no one in Israel have I found such faith" (Matthew 8:10). I wonder how often we find ourselves praising the faith of a Muslim, a Hindu, or a Buddhist.

This Gospel passage always brings to mind an experience I had shortly after being assigned to Thailand in early 1990. My intention was to work with people who have HIV and AIDS. I was only a month in the country, still in language school, and feeling the pressure at age fifty. To relax, I'd go out on weekends with my camera.

Near the Maryknoll house there was a small Buddhist monastery. Passing the gate on one of my excursions, I noticed a young monk nursing a baby gibbon with a bottle of milk. Unable to manage more than a greeting in Thai, I gestured that I wanted to take his picture. He smilingly agreed. I had only taken a shot or so when I felt a tap on my shoulder and turned to face another monk: "You summons to abbot's quarters," he said, rather sternly. "Follow me!"

From years of work in the Middle East, I realized that religious etiquette is easily breached; I was already framing an apology as I mounted the stairs to the room where the young abbot was seated cross-legged on a straw mat. I watched the monk prostrate himself three times, but I didn't know enough to do the same, though I had the presence of mind to doff my shoes before entering. "I am just new here," I stammered, hoping he might understand my English if I exaggerated each syllable, and spoke loudly. "And if I offended. . . ." He cut me off. "I am new here, too," he said softly, "a refugee from Burma." I was surprised at his command of English. A brief exchange, ended with, "It would be nice if you could teach the monks English." "Yes, well I can't really, at least not right now," I answered smiling and followed suit awkwardly as the monk who had accompanied me prostrated three times and we withdrew.

Two days later I brought the photographs to the monk caring for the gibbon, again only to be interrupted by a tap on my shoulder. "You summons to abbot's quarters." What followed was almost identical to the previous exchange of words, ending with, "It would be nice if you could teach the monks English." "Yes, well, I already said I can't," this time said without a smile.

The monks perhaps had observed where I lived while on their alms round, for I sometimes sat on the doorsteps with my morning coffee. We were at the supper when another member of the community remarked that a group of Buddhist monks was on the door stoop. I recognized the one who had tapped my shoulder and hastened to the door. "List of students and hours of teaching," he said, handing me a paper. "Oh, no," I replied. "You tell the abbot I can't do this. I've got language studies." "You tell him," the monk answered folding the paper. "Come!" "Keep my supper," I said over my shoulder, as I headed out the door in exasperation. This pesky abbot was proving a bit too pushy. My prostrations were curt. "I told you I can't teach the monks English. I'm in language school every day. And besides, you wouldn't want me teaching in your temple. I'm a Catholic missionary brother!" "What has that got to do with it?" he asked slowly. "I didn't ask you to teach us religion. We already have one. You will teach us English." "Why?" I almost shouted. He went on to explain that it would only be for three months, the period of the Buddhist rain retreat, the so-called Buddhist Lent. "Please." "Okay, an hour and a half a day only," I said breathing out audibly. "Tomorrow. Five o'clock you start," he answered.

I was there the next day just before five to find a monk waiting at the temple gate to lead me up to the awning-covered monastery roof where three rows of saffron-robed monks were installed on mats along with a whiteboard. No desks! I was to sit on the floor. Worse still, seated in the front row among the beaming young monks sat the young abbot. I raised my eyebrows in disbelief and sighed.

"My name is," I said, starting to write on the white board. . . . "Stop!" cried the abbot. My intuition was right: the man was going be a nuisance. "Now," he intoned, "In your country you had a great Negro leader . . ." I cut him off, "We don't use that word in my country," I replied with irritation, "We say African American."

"I don't care what word you use," he replied, bewildered, "I care that he was such a great, great leader. He was a leader from your religion, wasn't he? I read a small book about him in Burma and felt he was a great man. When the uprising took place for democracy, I thought I should try to do the same as him and so I led people from several of our villages in the marches for democracy for a number of weeks. At first we were filled with great hope—I was so happy. And then soldiers came, trucks filled with them and they shot the people in the streets and captured many others and took them away. We were in shock. I tried to keep those I led calm and organize groups to flee to the border. The jungle is thick and it was very difficult. Some were so weak. Five drowned crossing the swollen streams, as it was the rainy season. At the border we came under attack by Burmese army soldiers. We lost." He paused in silence. "Oh, don't say you lost," I mumbled, feeling lost as to what I could say, but he cut me off.

He went on, "Now, in the book I read about the American religious leader it said he sang a song with his people. Do you know it?" "Yes," I know it," I said, "We Shall Overcome." "Then teach it to us," he said softly, "It will be the first English lesson for these young monks. Buddhist monks," he added, "are not allowed by our monks' precepts to sing; but you will teach us this song and we will stand and sing, sing for those who died, and then we will never sing again for the rest of our life." And so it was that I taught a band of ragtag, barefoot refugee monks from Burma how to sing "We Shall Overcome." I was glad for the cover of nightfall on my way home because I could not hide the emotions on my face.

About three weeks after I started teaching English to the monks, the abbot called me aside after class. "I needed to know I could trust you," he said, "And I know I can. Come with me." He took me across the courtyard and opened the door to a large room under the worship hall. By the dim light of bare electric bulbs I made out long lines of people lying on mats with monks bent over them or kneeling to minister to them. "We carried the wounded with us," he said. They had heard I was a nurse. "Please help us." He went on to explain, "We are illegal and we are afraid they will put these people back to Burma if we take them to hospitals." It took me some while to convince him that this would not happen, and I was able, with the help of some of the monks, to get all of the patients attended to by Thai doctors and nurses.

Meanwhile we were busy trying to get UNHCR recognition for the refugees and worked on resettlement, and there were the continual protests and articles against the brutality of the Burmese military dictatorship and the imprisonment of countless political prisoners. The work at times seemed overwhelming, and at times I began to feel overwhelmed at the terrible injustice that was taking place. The monks always seemed calm and started to invite me to join in the chanting and meditation that took place in the evening before bedtime. It will bring you great inner peace, they assured me, it will teach you to let go. And so it did.

It was some time later that the newspapers reported that the recipients of the Nobel Peace Prize would jointly visited Thailand in support the imprisoned Burmese leader Aung San Su Kyi, who likewise had been awarded the Nobel Prize. Among them would be the Dalai Lama and Archbishop Desmond Tutu. When the abbot turned up with the clipping from the newspaper I assumed he was going to say something about the Dalai Lama and how a Buddhist monk had been so honored. Instead, he waved the clipping and said, "This leader for freedom, Desmond Tutu, is coming to Thailand. He is from your religion and you will arrange for him to come to our monastery to do a chanting ceremony with us and to pray a blessing for our people in Burma and Africa." "That's impossible!" I said. "I don't even know him. Get the Dalai Lama to come. He's from your religion." "No, he said, "I want to pray together with this Christian leader, Desmond Tutu."

"I don't think it can be done, but I'll try."

I contacted Maryknoll in New York, knowing that Orbis Books had had contact with Desmond Tutu and that he knew Maryknoll fairly well. I asked if there was any possible way to contact him to see if he might agree to meet with a Buddhist abbot, a refugee from Burma, who was keen to hold a religious service with him when he came to Bangkok. To my amazement he agreed, asked for a time and requested that he be picked up at the Anglican Church in Bangkok. It was the second time the abbot had me crying, as the two men, through interpreters, spoke of the importance of hope and the conviction that good triumphs over evil and their hope that all people may yet be free. After Buddhist chanting, a Christian blessing, and a hug between the two men, the abbot and the archbishop walked out of the worship hall hand in hand, both beaming.

Twenty years later on, I'm still learning from the monks, as I am sure they are from me. I have found Buddhists to be very open to me as a Christian. It is part of Lord Buddha's teaching: "Do not decry, deprecate, or condemn the religions of others. Honor whatever in them is worthy of honor. Listen, be curious, be willing to understand the doctrines of others."

I suspect, as a brother missioner, I sort of sensed the moment I walked through the gate of the monastery that I was coming home to brotherhood. Monks and brothers have more in common than might be imagined, just as do our Buddhist and Christian faiths.

Twenty-First Sunday in Ordinary Time

Fr. John McAuley, MM

Maryknoll, New York

Isaiah 22:15, 19–23; Psalm 138:1–3, 6, 8; Romans 11:33–36; Matthew 16:13–20

The Lord will fulfill his purpose for me; your steadfast love, O Lord, endures forever.   —*Psalm 138:8*

Paul today writes, "O the depth of the riches and wisdom and knowledge of God! How unsearchable are his judgments and how inscrutable his ways!" Yes indeed, God knows us, our histories, our sorrows and our joys, our failures and our successes better than we know ourselves, and certainly better than we know others. And, if reflective and honest, we also know that we are not always faithful: not always faithful to the measure of divinely planned stewardship we share over our own lives, over those placed closely in our lives, over our own society and its members and resources, and over the web of life and resources that make up our living planet. But God is always faithful; faithful, because of an all-encompassing love of us and of the sacred character of what is expressed in creation as a whole. Neither we nor creation are ever outside the divine embrace.

Genesis teaches that we share stewardship with God, but quickly reminds us of our weaknesses in that regard when left to ourselves. Ultimately, there is only one truly faithful steward, just as there is one Creator. And that ever-faithful Creator-Steward recovers and re-creates what is sometimes damaged or lost by us who share in the everyday, practical aspects of stewardship for persons, for life, and over resources.

The character of the stewardship of life and resources that we daily participate in is, ultimately, not one of merit and payments, though these have their place. Our stewardship is of the same character as the character of God's stewardship, i.e., based on inexplicable, inexhaustible love and care, and expressed in personal vulnerability and self-emptying.

The official Shebna, master of the palace, may not have been capable of exercising this style of authority in his stewardship. But the Lord was ever faithful, even in this particular situation of imbalance in stewardship. And through the Prophet Isaiah the Lord effected a rebalance.

Peter too, had to be rebalanced in the stewardship that he was given in today's Gospel. Jesus gave Peter a share in his own stewardship of care for those being gathered through Jesus' ministry. And yet, minutes later Jesus rebuked Peter for an exercise of his shared stewardship that was based on a character different from the one given by God to Jesus. And yet again, Jesus later had to once more rebalance the character of Peter's stewardship after the Resurrection, when he asked Peter three times "Do you love me?" and then recommissioned him.

There are a number of emerging situations in the world, some of them potentially disturbing to us, which may be fruitfully rethought in the light of today's readings. Among them is the growing economic power and influence of Asia. The emergence of Asia has many people unsettled, particularly the increasing influence of societies such as China and India, whose cultural and religious characters are so very different from ours—and in a few instances, even diametrically opposed to ours.

We should keep in mind that between these two countries alone there are over two billion people who until very recently lived in societies characterized by great poverty and very little social change. Along with the increase in wealth I have experienced in these societies, I have also seen many social developments and liberalizations that were undreamt of even a decade ago. Could it be that the Creator-Steward is stirring generative processes among those peoples, not necessarily deservedly or in a direct-payment response, but out of compassion for those straining under the heaviness of decades, even centuries, of poverty and stagnation? Yet, we may find ourselves in the same state of offended surprise that the people of Jesus' time experienced when he reminded a self-confident and proud nation that God sometimes acted decisively outside their society in cleansing an unbelieving leper, Namaan, while some in Israel remained unclean, and in coming to the assistance of a hungry, unbelieving widow of Zarepthath, while some in Israel continued to be hungry.

It may not be enough for the faithful Creator-Steward to have said on the lips of some, "O the depth of the riches and wisdom and knowledge of God! How unsearchable are his judgments and how inscrutable his ways!" God instead seems to wish that all peoples may also be able to echo Paul's subsequent words and say, "For from him and through him and to him are all things. To him be glory forever. Amen."

Twenty-Second Sunday in Ordinary Time

Marie Dennis, Maryknoll Affiliate

Washington, D.C.

Jeremiah 20:7–9; Psalm 63:2–6, 8–9; Romans 12:1–2; Matthew 16:21–27

If any want to become my followers, let them deny themselves and take up their cross and follow me.   —*Matthew 16:24*

Pictures of children climbing barren trees in a refugee camp and of hundreds of scrubby trees struggling to provide a modicum of shade for the poor huts that shelter exhausted families were common on the Internet during the Somali famine a few years ago. The pictures were poignant images of the important role that trees in East Africa play: as a community's meeting place where important decisions are made and where the process of community reconciliation can begin to unfold.

Trees are important throughout the Judeo-Christian tradition. In fact, near the beginning of the Bible is a description of the tree of life in the Garden of Eden, and near the end is a description of the tree of life on either side of the river, with its twelve kinds of fruit in the New Jerusalem.

In *Earth Community, Earth Ethics*, the theologian Larry Rasmussen writes about how a tree of life carries its community, providing homes and shelter, furniture, tools, boats, food and fuel, energy, and medicine. He reminds us that every single breath that every single human being has ever taken or will ever take depends on trees and on other green plants; all trees are literally trees of life. Trees, he writes, entertain journeys of the spirit. They are the subject of story and poetry and painting and sculpture; they are the site and substance of things religious. Trees join heaven and earth; they help us experience the fact that we are rooted in and are part of nature, even as we are constantly moving toward a horizon that is fullness of life.

In today's Gospel, Jesus turns toward Jerusalem where he will "undergo great suffering at the hand of the elders and chief priests and scribes, and be killed"—on a tree. Then he tells his friends, "If any want to become my followers, let them deny themselves and take up their cross and follow me."

What can that possibly mean in the context of a world where millions of children go to bed hungry every night and where trees are too often uprooted in the name of progress?

"And on the third day be raised": Jesus' death turned the cross back into a tree of life. By his death we know he overcame evil and reclaimed life, the life for which children in Somalia and Afghanistan and Haiti and so many other places in the world yearn, the life imagined as the New Jerusalem.

We are called to follow his lead. Perhaps the first step is to pay attention, to accompany all those whose lives are devastated by hunger and fear, to help carry the cross that is on their backs, to mourn with them in whatever ways we can.

When suffering assumes a scale so huge that the pain individuals or families suffer is subsumed into the wailing of a whole community, a whole country, an entire racial or cultural group, the soul of the human family is profoundly affected and the instinctive response of most people is what might be called social mourning. That is the first step, empathy and the charity it evokes.

But social mourning also has to move us to uproot social and ecological injustice. Global hunger has not just "happened." It is not an act of God for which we humans have no responsibility and over which we have no control. In fact, the war, climate change, rising food prices, and bad macroeconomic policies at the root of the hunger crises too often faced in different corners of the world are all evils that could have been overcome.

In a world that is so intensely interconnected, our carbon emissions, our trade policies, and our investment practices are intertwined with other root causes of serious hunger, even famine. To pick up a cross and follow Jesus may well mean that we feel so acutely the suffering of the children who are chronically hungry that we respond with both immediate generosity and a long-term commitment to understand and transform systemic roots of the famine.

Twenty-Third Sunday in Ordinary Time

Br. Martin Shea, MM

Guatemala

Ezekiel 33:7–9; Psalm 95:1–2, 6–9; Romans 13:8–10; Matthew 18:15–20

Love your neighbor as yourself.   *—Romans 13:9*

In today's reading Paul is having trouble with the Romans, just as he would have with us today, because people get caught up in what divides and separates them, in what causes war. We have to find what brings us together, and Paul helps us find that which we seek. It is love that fulfills the law, and the same love fulfills our lives.

The gap of separation closes when Jesus dares to touch the sick. With his touch healing takes place. Saint Francis of Assisi had a similar experience when he was able to bend down and kiss a leper. Dorothy Day joined the people on the street, and the Catholic Worker Movement was born. The missioner becomes one with the people he lives with. There is no distinction, no division. Even the doctors we work with here in Petén begin to become one with the people they serve. This is a struggle, because love is a struggle.

The struggle of love and peace-making in Guatemala continues after long years of a genocidal war that tore our poor country apart and ended in death and destruction, as all wars do. War is no answer. Paul, to the Romans and to us in the modern world, calls us back to the one answer—love—that transcends time and people. We all have within us that which can transform the world around us and within us. It can happen in our lives; it is happening in the lives of the Guatemalan people. As one young girl in our community put it, "No love, no peace."

This is not a popular message. It was not popular in the time of Jesus, and it is not popular in our time. But in a world of so much inhuman insanity of wars and violence, the message of Jesus and Paul is still the same and is still basic to our faith: peace is possible. It is not an easy message, but then no one ever said that to follow Jesus would be easy.

I would like to relate one story as I try to bring this reflection to some conclusion: There is a home for the aged here in Petén in this remote area of Guatemala, with some sixty-five men and women in the final years of their lives. I found myself going there regularly and just taking my place with them. In the beginning, it was very disconcerting, as there seemed to be separation between me and them, but over time the distance between us diminished. I now find myself to be one of them; we are all about the same age. Now that the distance between us has broken down, their presence and love helps me along the way. It is quite a surprise to find mission in an old plastic chair in a home for the aged!

Exaltation of the Holy Cross

Kathy McNeely, former Maryknoll lay missioner

Guatemala; Maryknoll Office for Global Concerns

Numbers 21:4–9; Psalm 78:1–2, 34–39; Philippians 2:6–11;
John 3:13–17

*I will utter dark sayings from of old, things that we have heard
and known, that our ancestors have told us.   —Psalm 78:2b–3*

We all have our stories. These stories are shaped by our cultural experience, by what our parents teach us, and by the way we choose to respond to the world around us. While living and working in Guatemala among indigenous Qeqchi' people, I heard stories that come to mind as I read today's readings for the celebration of the Exaltation of the Holy Cross.

Today's scriptures paint a picture of just how powerful stories can be—not only individual stories but the stories that an entire culture takes on. In the reading from Numbers we encounter the story that the Israelites told themselves while wandering in the desert. It was a hopeless story, filled with doom and despair. They had forgotten just how horrible their lives had been as slaves and demanded more comfort. They complained to Moses even about the manna that God gave them to survive: "Why have you brought us up out of Egypt to die in the wilderness? For there is no food and no water, and we detest this miserable food." As the expression of their misery grew, so did their troubles. Poisonous snakes bit people and left them to die. Through Moses, God invites the people to change their story from misery to gratitude, and in doing so, they are able to overcome their difficulties in the wilderness.

When I worked in San Luis, I met a young man, Norman, who lived with his wife, Dalia, and their three children in the neighborhood adjacent to mine. Norman asked me to come to his house the day his daughter Daisy was born. Dalia had never taken this long in labor with their other children. He worried that we might have to rush out to the clinic and he wanted me and the vehicle I drove nearby. Norman gave his six-year-old son a bit of money and asked him to go and buy some bread. When his son left, Norman said, "He's a bright boy. You watch, he's going to come back with bread." Then Norman confessed that he himself was never very bright. He said that when he was a boy, his mother would give him money to go to the store for a spool of thread, but we would go and come back with nothing because he had forgotten what his mother told him to buy.

This was Norman's story, a story of defeat, a story that indicated that Norman just did not measure up to others' expectations. His story was quite different from my experience of Norman. In community life he always had positive input that helped people make decisions, but since Norman didn't really believe in himself, he prefaced that input with "some people say" or some other indication that the thought he was contributing was not his own. In this way, he constantly reinforced his internal notion that his thoughts didn't matter.

In that respect, Norman was no different from many Guatemalans who, after decades of oppression, just did not believe in themselves as individuals. However, as I reflect back on my experience living and working in Guatemala, this individual story changes when a community decides to take action together. In this regard an expression from the ancient Mayan creation story in the *Popol Vuh* gives voice to the notion: "Everyone rises up and no one is left behind."

In the mid-1990s, the peace accords were signed and refugees began returning from Mexico to rebuild their lives. I remember how bleak the surroundings felt when a group of us drove into the camp. There were plastic tarps everywhere, a group of men were working together to chop fire wood, and women where lined up to gather water from one of two newly constructed wells. The ground was muddy from some of the first spring rains. When we spoke to Eduardo, one of the community leaders, he was completely animated. He talked about their move from Mexico and how they had formed committees to build and plant and help one another get settled into their new homes. He sat tall on his stool as he spoke with so much hope for the future that this community of refugees would build tighter.

Then we asked Eduardo about the circumstances under which he left Guatemala, when he fled to Mexico. Immediately his demeanor changed. His shoulders slumped, his voice got low and quiet. It crackled as he struggled not to cry. He spoke of an army raid on their village. He was just a nine-year-old boy; he fled with his mother and sister. There were family members, animals, possessions left behind; he could hear screaming and see flames coming from the rooftops of village houses when he looked back from the dark woods where they hid. Despite his temptation to stand and watch, he was pressed by the adults to keep moving.

The massacre story that caused Eduardo to flee is a crucifixion story. The feelings that welled up in Eduardo as he spoke could be compared to those experienced by Jesus' followers once he was crucified. After living through the suffering and horror that their dear friend experienced, they must have questioned how they would go on.

Yet, they did, and therein lies the mystery of how a story of devastating and paralyzing crucifixion becomes the exaltation of the holy cross. Somehow, surrounded by a community of survivors, Eduardo, like the followers of Jesus, could turn his story around. Destruction and death did not have the final word! With the commitment to come home to Guatemala and rebuild their lives, God's story of compassion, of great reversals could now be his. He now told a story of resurrection and new beginnings.

In a world that cries with signs of destruction and defeat, we are challenged to see the great reversal that is offered in the cross. Jesus "emptied himself, taking the form of a slave. . . . He humbled himself, and became obedient to the point of death—even death on a cross." But his death was not the final answer; the final story is a story of eternal life for those who chose to embrace it. Let us go out this week and tell new stories, stories that embrace the past but do not hold us there, stories that promise new life and invite us to create a future full of life-giving possibilities.

Twenty-Fifth Sunday in Ordinary Time

Sr. Luise Ahrens, MM

Cambodia

Isaiah 55:6–9; Psalm 145:2–3, 8–9, 17–18; Philippians 1:20–24, 27; Matthew 20:1–16

For my thoughts are not your thoughts, nor are your ways my ways, says the Lord.   —Isaiah 55:8

Today's readings give us one clear, hard fact to explore: "God's not our kind of folks," a confession, or lament, that comes from a black woman of great faith who looks at the Bible and at the world around her (*God on Our Minds*, Liturgical Press, 1982). Amazingly enough, God is not made in my image and likeness but rather we, we hope, are made in God's.

The first reading gives us the clue about what is coming. Isaiah 55:8–9 says, "For my thoughts are not your thoughts, nor are your ways my ways, says the Lord. For as the heavens are higher than the earth, so are my ways higher than your ways and my thoughts than your thoughts."

"God's not our kind of folks" rings true when we look at the world around us. God is, as we see in the Bible, "other." In Matthew, chapter 5, the Beatitudes do not image a God who is like us: "Blessed are those who are persecuted for righteousness' sake." The passage does not read: How happy are you, you with your comfortable Christian life. No, what God calls happiness seems to be out of reach: to be gentle, merciful, and pure in heart, a fighter for justice.

The psalmist picks up this difference between us and God but as a fact, a reality to be praised. "Great is the Lord, and greatly to be praised; his greatness is unsearchable" (Psalm

145:3). Recognizing the very otherness of God, we are called
to give thanks for God's greatness. We cannot know God in
all of God's magnificence, but we do know, once again from
the psalm, that "the Lord is near to all who call . . . who call
on him in truth." In our lives every single day there are gifts
and challenges that turn us to God, to call out for help, to give
thanks, to lament or to rejoice. The only need for us who are
called Christians is that we turn to God.

The Gospel reading is the clearest example of God's difference from us. Each of us has read that Gospel and felt a clear
identity with the workers who had been out in the fields (or on
the construction site, or in the garment factory) for the entire
day. They were standing in line for their wages, seeing the
reward given to the latecomers and thinking to themselves:
Surely I will get more; I deserve it more than these folks who
came in the last hour of work. And yet, the owner gives them
the same amount, the same amount as me, and I worked so
hard! What does this say about me? What does it say about the
owner of the field?

It speaks about me: In the world of work, I expect to receive
what is due to me—to do my work, get my salary and maybe
even a bonus at the end of the year. Do I feel that way in my
spiritual life? Do I expect God to daily punish my weakness,
my frailty, my sin; do I hope for "justice" in this realm as well,
getting back what I have given? Probably not. Rather, each
of us hopes for, prays for, the unbounded generosity of God
to cover our sins with love and forgiveness, to manifest the
unbounded generosity we expect in our God.

In Cambodia, where I live and work, we have a project
that prevents HIV transmission from mother to child, and it
works: the children are free of the virus. The old wisdom said
that HIV negative children of HIV positive women should

not nurse, but most new research says that if new mothers are on the drugs and if they have good nutrition, 95 percent of children will not get AIDS from nursing. We can provide powdered milk for $26,000 per year. What more can we do for these mothers if that money is not spent on prevention against a 5 percent chance of contracting AIDS? We struggle with these questions, and we struggle as well with those of lifesaving but very expensive surgeries for some very poor people: How much do we spend to save the one? How much is left in the pot for the many?

These are our kind of limits—of resources, of choices—and they are real, but God is not like us. There is no limit on God or on God's love. As the owner of the field says to the complaining workers, "Am I not allowed to do what I choose with what belongs to me?" Our task is to trust in God's love for each one of us, not limiting God to our puny stature but rejoicing in the God whose generosity fills us again and again to overflowing, pressed down and running over.

Twenty-Sixth Sunday in Ordinary Time

Fr. Paul Masson, MM

El Paso/Ciudad Juárez

Ezekiel 18:25–28; Psalm 25:4–9; Philippians 2:1–11 or 2:1–5; Matthew 21:28–32

Let each of you look not to your own interests, but to the interests of others. —Philippians 2:4

In the Gospel, Jesus presents the parable of the two sons. When the father asked the first son to work in the vineyard, he said no, but later changed his mind and went. The second answered yes, that he would go, but he did not. The setting of this Gospel is very important. Jesus was talking with the chief priests and the elders who were questioning his authority: "When [Jesus] entered the temple, the chief priests and the elders of the people came to him as he was teaching, and said, 'By what authority are doing these things?'"

Jesus compares the two sons with two groups of people: the authorities and the outcasts. The first son is like the outcast—a tax collector or a prostitute—who will enter the kingdom of God before the chief priests and the elders.

Jesus goes on to say to the authorities, "For John came to you in the way of righteousness and you did not believe him, but the tax collectors and the prostitutes believed him; and even after you saw it, you did not change your minds and believe him."

The way of righteousness was shown to me by the mother of Esmeralda Herrera. Esmeralda and her mother lived near one of the chapels where Maryknoll served in Ciudad Juárez, Chihuahua, Mexico, across the river from El Paso, Texas, where I lived from 1998 until 2008. In the past couple of decades, this area has experienced a reign of terror that has moved from subtle to explicit. Starting in 1994, mutilated bodies of murdered young women were found in the desert around the city. In November 2001, the bodies of two young women were found in a cotton field within the city. One of the victims was Esmeralda; she was fourteen years old. Within a few days, the police found six more bodies in the cotton field, women of different ages who died at different times.

As you can imagine, this was a very difficult time for Esmer alda's mother. Despite her job loss and the difficulty of raising a family, she did not relent in looking for justice and answers to her questions. She found none. Among many of the families of the disappeared and murdered women, it was common to hear complaints about the police, the authorities, even God. As expressed in the first reading from Ezekiel: "Yet you say, 'The way of the Lord is unfair.'" While we tried to accompany Esmeralda's mother, we encountered silence; little by little we put this reality out of our thoughts and minds, and life went on.

By 2008, it was obvious that the city was out of control and that the dark forces of evil ruled the day. The violence began to escalate to a point that almost all of the neighbors experienced some type of extortion, many through kidnappings or assassinations. Few signs of hope and change were seen.

However, in June 2011, a Movement for Peace with Justice and Dignity was organized by Mexican poet Javier Sicilia, whose twenty-four-year-old son, Juan Francisco, was assassinated along with six other people near Cuernavaca in March 2011. The movement calls for an end to the militarization of the country and to the drug war, a reform of the federal laws for workers, and a reform of the national security law of Mexico.

Javier Sicilia held public discussions with the authorities, even with then President Felipe Calderon, and, as part of the movement, arranged a "Caravan for Peace" which has traveled throughout the country, visiting many of the cities most affected by drug-related violence.

In June 2011, the Caravan for Peace (also called "Caravana del Consuelo," Caravan of Consolation) visited Ciudad Juárez, which Javier Sicilia referred to as the "epicenter of pain." According to a report from the Workers Pastoral Office of the Diocese of Ciudad Juárez, "Hundreds of victims came out of their anonymity and gathered with hundreds of the inhabitants of a victimized city, human rights activists and community organizers, workers, students, and artists. With each testimonial and each cry for justice, everybody cried out in solidarity: 'You are not alone, you are not alone.'"

In the reading from Ezekiel we hear, "When the wicked turn away from the wickedness they have committed and do what is lawful and right, they shall save their life." To understand the evil that we live within our world today, it is necessary to reflect on our present reality. Many people see the problems of drug-related violence in Mexico as a problem of Mexico alone. This ignores the reality that Mexico and the United States are very much interrelated. The economic chaos in Mexico has been, in many ways, the result of the so-called free trade agreement, the North American Free Trade Agreement (NAFTA). Also, the drug cartels are in business because of the huge profits that are made in the sale of illegal drugs by and to people in our country. Guns that kill people in Mexico are arms that are bought in the United States.

The Movement for Peace with Justice and Dignity invites people throughout the world to join in an awareness of the need for solidarity and justice. It invites us to say that we care and that the victims are not alone. If we want to follow the path of righteousness today, we have to follow people like the mother of Esmeralda and the poet Javier Sicilia.

Twenty-Seventh Sunday in Ordinary Time

Kathy Morefield, Maryknoll Affiliate

Cambodia

Isaiah 5:1–7; Psalm 80:9, 12–16, 19–20; Philippians 4:6–9; Matthew 21:33–43

Whatever is true, whatever is honorable, whatever is just, whatever is pure, whatever is pleasing, whatever is commendable, if there is any excellence and if there is anything worthy of praise, think about these things. —*Philippians 4:8*

Who does this earth belong to? In this era of globalization and migration, to whom does the vineyard belong? In the first reading from Isaiah, we hear that "the vineyard of the Lord of hosts is the house of Israel, and the people of Judah are his pleasant planting; he expected justice, but saw bloodshed; righteousness, but heard a cry!"

A Jewish friend once told me that Jews believe their purpose in life is to help God repair the world. Indeed, the prophet Isaiah proclaimed to the people of Israel, "You shall raise up the foundations of many generations; you shall be called the repairer of the breach, the restorer of streets to live in" (Isaiah 58:12).

They were familiar words to the people of Israel, yet the audience in today's Gospel story—made up of the Pharisees, elders, and leaders of the Temple—did not heed its message. Rather than raise the people up, they loaded them down with heavy burdens, making their lives even more miserable. What does the parable say about leaders of nations and institutions today? How are the leaders of the world caring for, raising up, and restoring God's creation in the twenty-first century? In the vineyard of Cambodia, the gap between the rich and the poor grows alarmingly wider each year.

Desperately poor people are forced out of their meager homes, which are sold to wealthy developers for large sums of money. Slums are burned and bulldozed, and the people scatter in fear for their lives. The evicted, many of whom owned their small houses, are often relocated to camps far outside the cities where there is no running water, no sewage treatment, no schools or transportation, and where they are cut off from their sources of income in the city. The very people entrusted to raise them up and ensure their well-being have squandered their trust.

Where is the hope? My husband discovered a new Khmer (Cambodian) restaurant in Phnom Penh. The traditional food was healthy and delicious, but it was the working conditions that excited him. The restaurant was started by a husband and wife with a mission to recruit poor women from the countryside and raise them up. In Cambodia, as in most places in the world, there is little regard for the poor and unfortunate, especially women. In most Khmer restaurants, the kitchen and waitstaff are underpaid, overworked, and often abused. They work long hours seven days a week for less than poverty wages.

At the new restaurant, however, the workers are paid a fair wage, and at the end of each month the proceeds are divided equally among the staff, including the owners. The two chefs are women, unheard of in most Khmer restaurants. In order to avoid corruption, the restaurant will not hire family members of the staff or owners. Workers are cared for when they are ill and do not lose income for sick days. The staff meets every week to talk over problems and finds ways to resolve issues that arise. They keep a donation box and decide as a group how to share the collected revenue with those in need.

Somnang, the owner, calls himself a peacemaker and told us that he was inspired by the life of Mahatma Gandhi and his work for justice and equality. There is no income gap between Somnang, his wife, Bopha, and the rest of the staff. Everyone works hard to ensure that the restaurant is a success. Everyone is a stakeholder.

Because of its delicious food, excellent service, and friendly atmosphere, the restaurant has become popular with government officials and workers at the nearby Ministry of Education. Perhaps the vision of Somnang and Bopha will inspire both them and others to share the bounty of God's creation.

" 'The stone that the builders rejected has become the cornerstone; this was the Lord's doing, and it is amazing in our eyes.' Therefore I tell you, the kingdom of God will be taken away from you and given to a people that produces the fruits of the kingdom."

Twenty-Eighth Sunday in Ordinary Time

Fr. Dennis Moorman, MM

Brazil

Isaiah 25:6–10; Psalm 23; Philippians 4:12–14, 19–20;
Matthew 22:1–14 or 22:1–10

*On this mountain the Lord of hosts will make for all peoples a
feast of rich food, a feast of well-aged wines, of rich food filled
with marrow, of well-aged wines strained clear." —Isaiah 25:6*

The prophet Isaiah presents a celestial vision of salvation where
God prepares a rich banquet for all peoples, where death will
be destroyed forever, and the tears and shame of the suffering
peoples will be wiped away for good. As Christians, when we
pray the great prayer that Jesus taught us, we say, "Thy kingdom come, thy will be done, on earth as it is in heaven." This
phrase sums up our work as Christians: to make this vision of
heaven a reality here on earth.

While working in Brazil as a missioner, I had a special pastoral outreach to sexual and gender minorities. One night as we
were attending a workshop on human rights, one of the young
transgendered persons who had been expected to participate
did not show up. The next morning we found out why. The
battered body of Mauro was found thrown away like trash in a
darkened alley. Mauro was such a gentle soul who would never
hurt anyone. Nobody could figure out why someone would
make such a brutal attack on such a kind and peaceful person.
Even more disturbing was that a giant cross was carved into
Mauro's thorax and neck, seemingly justifying the killing for
some sort of religious reason.

Ironically, this violent act motivated the sexual and gender minority communities to come together and organize

themselves to demand respect for their human rights. Often-times, when they would go to the police to report a crime, they would be heckled and abused by the very police officers that were supposed to be equally protecting all citizens. As a result of their organized efforts in response to Mauro's violent death, a special office at the police station was opened to receive sexual and gender minorities who had their human rights violated. All police officers working in this office had special sensitivity training to assure that anyone entering this office would feel safe and protected.

When I preached at Mauro's Mass of Resurrection, I tried to make sense of the cross that was found carved into Mauro's body. I said that by no means does this symbol of the cross indicate that our Christian faith justifies such violence for any reason. But rather, the cross that was carved on Mauro's body served as a sign that Jesus Christ is still suffering today in the broken and battered bodies of our brothers and sisters who undergo violence due to their sexual orientation and gender identification. For us Christians, the cross is a sign of hope amid great suffering. And the hope that came from Mauro's terrible death was the masses of people uniting in outrage and working to make their community a more accepting place for those who are different from the majority and who often suffer violence because of it.

In today's Gospel from Matthew, Jesus tells a parable to the religious authorities where he compares the kingdom of heaven to a king who threw a great wedding feast for his son and sent out invitations for people to attend. An interesting twist in the story comes when the king notices a guest attending the feast who was not wearing a wedding garment. In anger, the king has this disrespectful guest thrown out. The lack of a wedding garment indicates the hypocrisy of the guest who came to the feast with the wrong intentions. Church should be a place where all peoples are welcomed, but unfortunately, many people often feel excluded by a hypocritical church.

What would our church and world look like if we truly learned to accept and celebrate the beauty of diversity, rather than judge and condemn others who are different from the majority? The prophet Isaiah describes this heavenly vision as "a feast of rich food, a feast of well-aged wines, of rich food filled with marrow, of well-aged wines strained clear." How delicious, sensuous and joyous! This is what the kingdom of heaven is like. To enter the feast, we have only to accept the invitation with a pure intention, void of any hypocrisy.

Twenty-Ninth Sunday in Ordinary Time

Cecelia Aguilar Ortiz, former Maryknoll lay missioner

Thailand

Isaiah 45:1, 4–6; Psalm 96:1, 3–5, 7–10; First Thessalonians 1:1–5; Matthew 22:15–21

O sing to the Lord a new song; sing to the Lord, all the earth. Declare his glory among the nations, his marvelous works among all the peoples. —Psalm 96:1, 3

Today's Gospel reading is filled with much drama. We see Pharisees and Herodians, unlikely political bedfellows, set out to trap Jesus (with flattery no less) over the question of taxes. The issue of taxes was no small matter. The Jewish community, weighed down by the oppression of the Roman Empire and its system of taxation, had experienced ongoing calls for revolution by the nationalists of the day. The Pharisees and Herodians on one hand, and the crowds following Jesus on the other, want to know where Jesus stands on this issue: submit to Rome or challenge Rome's authority? By asking his adversaries to produce the very coin used to pay the tax, Jesus reveals their hypocrisy in carrying such a coin into the Temple. But Jesus' final statement, "Give therefore to the emperor the things that are the emperor's, and to God the things that are God's," leaves them astounded as they walk away.

It is the phrase "[Give] to God the things that are God's" that brings this debate to a whole new level. Jesus and his followers know "the earth is the Lord's and all that is in it" (Psalm 24:1). This is not about an easy separation between religion and politics. This is about understanding the right relationship between God and all of creation. Everything is of God and, we are called to live in such a way that honors this profound truth.

This view of God and the whole of creation is common among the indigenous people who reside in the mountainous areas across Southeast Asia. The Karen people are one of the many groups of indigenous or "hill tribe" people, as they are called in Thailand, who for centuries have subsisted on the land, especially the mountainous, forested areas. Although the majority of the Karen people reside in Burma, over 300,000 Karen live in parts of northern and western Thailand.

In Thailand, the hill tribe people are considered backward for maintaining their traditional ways and are accused of destroying the forest through the use of slash and burn farming methods. In reality, the Karen have promoted sustainable agricultural practices that honor and protect the diversity of the ecological system in which they live. If you look at any map of Thailand, you will see that the most pristine forest remaining is located in the areas traditionally populated by the Karen people. After almost a century of rapid industrial development and a switch from subsistence farming to large-scale agricultural production for export, over 80 percent of Thailand's forests have been destroyed. This model of development, which uses up the earth's natural resources for economic gain, is in direct contradiction to the traditional ways of the Karen.

In the Karen worldview, God, the human person and community, and nature are all intrinsically connected and interdependent. They believe that as long as people live in harmony with each other and nature, God will provide everything they need, particularly a good harvest. The Karen depend on the forest for their livelihood. Rice is their "daily bread" and the cultivation of rice is a sacred practice. The Karen practice a type of rotational farming in which an area of land is cultivated and then left to lie fallow for seven years. This method does not deplete the land of its nutrients and allows for regeneration of the forest as the community moves from one space to another from year to year. This farming method requires large land areas in order to provide enough food for the community and to allow the land to regenerate. This has created conflict between the Karen and government forestry officials who want to "preserve" the forest by displacing the indigenous communities and converting the area to national parks, which unfortunately have been poorly managed, leading to ongoing deforestation and misuse of the protected lands.

For decades, leaders from the Karen community and other hill tribe groups have been creating networks to help each other preserve and support their traditional ways of living off the land. With rice as a bond and a common worldview that understands what it means to give back to God what is God's, these communities are using their local wisdom to protect their environment and to discuss with the government their traditional methods. They are teaching their children to respect their heritage and to find ways to engage in the mainstream society without losing their customs and traditions.

Jesus' message in today's Gospel of living in right relationship with God and all of creation is being handed down by the Karen community from generation to generation in the midst of great adversity. It is also reiterated by Pope Benedict in his 2010 World Day of Peace message, "If You Want to Cultivate Peace, Protect Creation." In it he states, "The quest for peace by people of good will surely would become easier if all acknowledge the indivisible relationship between God, human beings and the whole of creation." This truly is the challenge of our times.

Thirtieth Sunday in Ordinary Time

Judy Coode

Maryknoll Office for Global Concerns

Exodus 22:20–26; Psalm 18:2–4, 47, 51; First Thessalonians
1:5–10; Matthew 22:34–40

*Do not mistreat or oppress a resident alien, for you were aliens
in Egypt.*   —*Exodus 22:21*

In January 2013, the board of commissioners of Carroll
County, Maryland, voted unanimously to make English the
county's official language. Supporters of the measure clearly
state that they want to ensure that undocumented migrants
know that they are not welcome in that jurisdiction. Mission
accomplished.

Carroll is the third county in Maryland to pass an "English
only" ordinance and is one of dozens—if not hundreds—of
local governments in the United States to pass such a rule.

What is the source of this, this fear of diversity, this need to
establish symbolic walls? How can many people who consider
themselves Christian listen to readings such as the ones today
from Exodus and Matthew and still justify their xenophobic
actions?

Jesus tells us the second great commandment is to love our
neighbors as ourselves. How much do we love ourselves? Do
we fully recognize our own worth, the fact that we are truly
beloved by God, that our existence is woven into the life force
of all the rest of creation? God's enduring love, knitted into all
living things, created us, sustains us, heals us, and binds us to
one another. When we lose touch with that connection, fear
and distrust bleed in.

At a church in my neighborhood, dozens of adults, mostly from Central America, gather on weeknights for English classes. There is great love in the hallways at this little school, held in the same building as Sunday morning catechism classes. Posters designed for children's religious education instruction line the walls—Jesus with the lambs, St. Francis with the birds, Mary at Fatima.

The people in these classes are from Mexico, Guatemala, El Salvador, Honduras, and a few are from African countries: Cote D'Ivoire, Mali. . . . One regular student is a woman from Haiti. They are eager and motivated to learn, and they give complete trust to the volunteer teachers who try to help them navigate the choppy waters of English grammar and pronunciation.

Their reason for attending the classes usually is "I need a better job," though one man said he hoped to improve his English so that he could understand his children, born in the United States and currently in elementary school. The construction workers, hotel maids, and kitchen hands listen and read and write, and strive to be good neighbors in their adopted country.

Though we don't often feel it and sometimes would like to reject the idea, we are connected to all. Our love for ourselves should be healthy and strong, and it should be extended into our love for others. We must be valiant in our efforts to keep fear and distrust at bay. We must trust in God's overwhelming love for us and recognize that that same love is extended to all.

All Saints' Day

Liz Mach, Maryknoll lay missioner

Tanzania

Revelation 7:2–4, 9–14; Psalm 24:1–6; First John 3:1–3;
Matthew 5:1–12

Blessed are the meek, for they will inherit the earth. Blessed are those who hunger and thirst for righteousness, for they will be filled.   —Matthew 5:5–6

Today all around the world we remember our saints. These can be those who are famous and well known for their deeds, whose stories we have read throughout our lives and who we try to emulate. Their stories have remained in our collective memory. Our saints can also be those who only few of us know and respect but are the ones we often remember today. These are the people who have influenced our lives and made an impact on the direction we choose to continue in our life's path. It is often in their simplicity that we find our own road. They are our mothers and fathers, friends, and co-workers who have lived good and faithful lives. We know who they are and we hold them in our hearts.

Today's Gospel reading, from the Sermon on the Mount, is truly the most simple and yet profound teaching that we have to follow to live these good and faithful lives. Being merciful, hungering and thirsting for righteousness, being a peacemaker are simple ways to follow Jesus each day in our encounters with each other and therefore are the ways to inherit God's kingdom. For many of us, these are also very difficult guidelines to follow in our daily lives. We want to be peacemakers, to be merciful to those we meet along the way each day and yet we stumble and let so many other distractions interfere with our journey toward God and care of our neighbor.

More realistically, we are challenged by these readings when we reflect on the issues surrounding immigration in the world today. So many nations are faced with the difficulty of their neighbors being in civil unrest that is forcing men, women, and children to leave their homes and travel great distances by foot to find safety in another country. Faced with all of this uncertainty, the worst thing for them is to find a border closed, to be unwelcomed and not allowed to enter into safety. Women give birth along the journey, children die from hunger and thirst, and parents are unable to provide for their families. Desperation and hopelessness overwhelm them. An uncertain future looms before them. The message from Jesus' teaching of the Beatitudes is needed today now more than ever to be shouted from the mountaintops.

Africa continues to struggle with drought, migration, and civil unrest. We, in the United States, are not on the border of these countries, so often we can lament that others should be welcoming those who are fleeing the war, or we can simply ignore what is happening because it is so far away from our own reality. Yet, we have our issues on our own borders, and our first response is often to close the door on those who are searching for a better life for their families. What would Jesus' response have been? How would he have taught us to be more welcoming and generous to those in need of our help? How would he have let us know who our neighbors are?

I do think his response to issues of migration could be deciphered through his teaching on the Beatitudes. Jesus' way was simply to have each individual reflect on his or her own questions. When am I not meek? When do I not practice peacemaking? How am I not merciful to others? As I reflect on these issues I can then dig deeper into my own responses to those who are knocking on our borders and asking for help. Am I responding in the way Jesus wants me to respond? Am I placing my own fears on the frontline rather than welcoming with my heart?

Immigration is a worldwide issue. Refugees and displaced people can challenge even the most open and welcoming person when their own lifestyle is put into question. Migration can need long-term responses from each one of us as the world becomes smaller and travel more routine. Reaching out and welcoming another when it could affect our own lifestyle can be difficult. How would the saints of yesterday and the saints of today respond? How do we reflect and respond? What is my response? Amen.

All Souls' Day

Bertha Haas, Maryknoll lay missioner

Tanzania

Wisdom 3:1–9 or 3:1–6, 9; Psalm 27:1, 4, 7–9, 13–14;
Romans 6:3; Matthew 25:31–46

*The souls of the righteous are in the hand of God . . . God tested
them and found them worthy of himself. . . . They will shine
forth, and will run like sparks through the stubble.*
                                                   —*Wisdom 3:1, 5, 7*

Today's readings exhort us to a faith and hope that turn things
topsy-turvy. In the eyes of many, the children with disabilities
whom we serve at Huruma School are afflicted, are a punishment to their families. They are often regarded as *mizigo*, or
baggage. But as we see them at Huruma, they are already shining. They may not be able to walk or speak clearly, but their
personalities sparkle, as contagious as sparks in dry stubble.

When a neighbor visited sixteen-year-old Halima, who lives
with cerebral palsy, at school waving gaily at guests and dancing with her classmates—yes, in her wheelchair—she could not
believe this was the same child she had seen isolated in a dark
room at home.

Enoch and Edward are nine years old and had attended
other schools before coming to Huruma. Similar disabilities
have drawn them together. Their joy in each other permeates
their classroom. Enoch is so pleased to be at Huruma where
he says "no one is afraid of me." At his prior school his classmates would run away from him because in his unsteadiness
he would sometimes grab a classmate's arm to steady himself. Since neither Enoch nor Edward is steady on his feet,
they enjoy racing against each other. If they fall, they get up
and run on, confident that classmates will cheer them on, a

confidence as strong and as comforting as the comforting confidence we are urged to have in God.

I am struck by the phrase from the book of Wisdom: "run like sparks through stubble." What an image of resurrection! Traditionally in Tanzania, ancestors are an important part of the family. Ancestors are to be honored. One's behavior is to be true to their values. In turn, the ancestors protect the community. So All Souls' Day is very important, overshadowing All Saints' Day. After the Jumuiya (small Christian communities) spend several days cleaning the cemetery, the parish gathers there for Mass the evening of November 2. Those preparing for baptism and confirmation—children, youth, and adults— are especially encouraged to participate in the preparation and the celebration as a sign that they are willing to join fully in the work of the community. In the Mass the entire community, the living and the ancestors, join together in this great act of worship. All the choirs unite signifying the importance of this feast.

Today's readings can be an avenue of healing, a source of new life, for a family that has lost a loved one whose life brought shame or trouble to the family. Daudi's father was an alcoholic who died during a night of drunken wandering. The reading from Wisdom has given Daudi, a young adult, a new image of his father. His father's alcoholism was a trial through which he was "found worthy" of God. It was an affliction that Baba (the loved father) was unable to cast off in this life. But Baba is now free from this affliction. Having received grace and mercy, he now runs like sparks through stubble, igniting flames of love. Believing that Baba is now finally at peace, Daudi has been able to pull firmly to his bosom Baba's values: forgiveness, unity within the family, talking out problems that may arise.

Truly, death is not the end. Rather, it is the beginning of a new life, a resurrection, not only for the deceased, but for those who mourn as well.

Thirty-Second Sunday in Ordinary Time

Fred Goddard, former Maryknoll lay missioner

Philippines

Wisdom 6:12–16; Psalm 63:2–8; First Thessalonians 4:13–18 or 4:13–14; Matthew 25:1–13

Wisdom is radiant and unfading, and she is easily discerned by those who love her, and is found by those who seek her.
                                                                  —Wisdom 6:12

Today's first reading gives us advice not only for listening to the rest of the readings, but even how to live our lives: "To fix one's thought on [wisdom] is perfect understanding, and one who is vigilant on her account will soon be free from care." It begins with the obvious theme of this day and this season—be alert, be awake, and be ready—but also a less obvious theme, that of seeking an encounter with God and with others.

One can reflect on these readings and on other readings at this time with respect to the ultimate encounter with God in heaven. Referring to the parable of the ten bridesmaids, the Gospel states, "The kingdom of heaven will be like this." However, this idea of being alert to God's coming does not mean a passive watching and waiting, but a call to an active engagement in the world.

The wedding was an important symbol to Jesus in this parable as well as the earlier parable in Matthew of the wedding banquet. Perhaps both parables came out of Jesus' own experiences of going to weddings, such as the one at Cana. For myself, my own wedding was the most important experience in my life.

In the Gospel readings, one can interpret the weddings or wedding banquets as a culminating event. For my wife,

Jeanette, and me, it was just the beginning. The theme for our ceremony in the Philippines was "partners in mission." It was an opportunity to recommit ourselves to God's mission, this time as a couple.

Our commitments were not limited to our vows to one another, though. We also called forth the community to participate with us in creating a better world. Our vows to the community read, "Embodied in our commitment to one another is a renewed faith commitment, a call to mission.

"We dedicate our lives to the continued struggle for social transformation, to witness to and work with you in achieving the dreams of future generations. We shall be with you in times of despair and in times of hope, in times of struggle and in times of celebration."

The community then responded by reading: "As your fellow believers and All Souls, we pledge our commitment to the same mission. We will do what God requires of us: 'to do what is just, to show constant love, and to walk humbly with our God.'"

Seen in this light, Christ is calling us to be alert, awake, and prepared to join in at the wedding table where we make our mutual commitment with God and with one another. That is why we must be prepared. That is why we must have our oils to keep our flame alive. It is a flame of passion for justice.

Returning to the Wisdom reading and the importance of the encounter, the readings speak to our encounter with God and with wisdom. Again, we can interpret that to be the encounter at the end of time, or we can view it as the encounter to which wisdom refers as she "appears to them in their paths." So the readings call us to be alert and awake to the day-to-day encounters. Not being ready and prepared may mean we miss those encounters.

In mission, and in this increasingly globalized world, those are often cross-cultural encounters, encounters with other faiths and other religions. Are they, too, welcome to the wedding feast? In the case of our wedding, they were more than welcome; they were invited to give a blessing,

In our work in Mindanao in the southern Philippines, we neither saw our commitment limited to the Catholic base Christian communities nor chose to work in isolation from other faiths. My wife's work with preschool children included centers in tribal areas, where the people retained many elements of their indigenous religions, and in Muslim communities. My own work and faith were enhanced by working alongside and with Mennonites, Lutherans, and other mission communities striving for peace and justice during the violence of the 1980s.

We felt the need to acknowledge this in our wedding, too, where we asked for a Catholic, Mennonite, tribal, and Muslim blessing as a closing to the celebration. Ironically, our Muslim friend could not find the church as we forgot to give her directions, assuming she knew where it was. So even in our own attempts to be alert and awake to interfaith encounters, we were still learning our own lessons!

Thirty-Third Sunday in Ordinary Time

Sr. Helen Graham, MM

Philippines

Proverbs 31:10–13, 19–20, 30–31; Psalm 128:1–5; First Thessalonians 5:1–6; Matthew 25:14–30 or 25:14–15, 19–20

For you are all children of light and children of the day; we are not of the night or of darkness.   —First Thessalonians 5:5

The aunt of a friend of mine had a jewelry business in the province about a two-hour ride south of Manila. When I visited, I spent one whole day just captivated watching the process by which a man's ring was produced. The process began at 8 a.m. with the firing and melting of a gold nugget, to shaping it into the form of a ring, to its hardening, and finally, by 5 p.m., the setting of gemstones in place to make a finished ring ready for the man who ordered it. This woman had a business in her home with a workshop where craftsmen were busy fashioning various types of jewelry. Her entrepreneurship reminds me of the wise woman in today's first reading who managed her household with skill, economic talent, and personal virtue. She certainly was someone who "[looked] well to the ways of her household, and [did] not eat the bread of idleness." Consequently her children "call her happy," and her husband "praises her." She has no fear for her household, rising "while it is still night and provides food for her household."

Psalm 128, which serves as a response for this reading, presumes that the entrepreneurial character is the man of the house! The woman is pictured not in terms of production but of reproduction: "Your wife will be like a fruitful vine within your house; your children will be like olive shoots around your table." In Philippine culture it is, very often, the woman who is the skillful one who manages the family economics with grace and strength. Surely the woman in the first reading presents a different picture than that of the Gospel man who received the one talent and, out of fear of the master, buried it in a napkin because he knew that the master was a harsh man, reaping where he did not sow, and gathering where he did not scatter seed. The fearful man's talent was not only unproductive but depreciated in value in the meantime. When the master returned he asked for an accounting, and the fearful man, who had nothing to show, was judged severely.

While the fearful man of the Gospel is condemned for his fear, the capable wife of Proverbs 31:10 is lauded as someone who is to be praised because she "fears the Lord." The responsorial psalm was probably chosen because it does indeed offer praise for the one "who fears the Lord, who walks in God's ways." The psalm considers such a one "happy," or "blessed," or "fortunate."

The Hebrew phrase "fear of the Lord" is often misunderstood, especially by those who use it to give a distorted picture of the "God of the Old Testament." Today's readings present us with two types of fear. The fearful man of the Gospel expresses an immobilizing type of fear that rendered him incapable of productive action, preventing him from investing his one talent. By the way, one talent was no small amount: D. J. Harrington, in his commentary on Matthew, suggests that "it was a large sum (like a 'million dollars' or 'a huge amount' in modern speech)." The woman of strength was praised because she "feared the Lord." Such a fear arises out of a profound awe and love that makes one concerned lest one bring displeasure to the beloved, who in this case is God.

The first and third readings allow us to reflect on the economy, providing images of a God-fearing woman who is economically productive, and a servile servant who is exceedingly fearful and, therefore, totally unproductive. These readings of the final weeks of Ordinary Time, however, also direct attention to the theme of eschatology (the final things), a theme that will figure prominently during the coming season of Advent. The Gospel passage has its own peculiar meaning within the context of Matthew where it is the third in a series of parables dealing with attitudes and behavior. Most often this eschatological dimension is overlooked by what Harrington calls the "usual moralizing approach" that results from the translation of the Greek unit of coinage, *talanton*, as "talent" understood as an ability or capacity. We are told to use our talents to the best of our ability thus failing to take into account "the eschatological horizon that is essential to the parable," which highlights the return of the master and the accounting. The Matthean version, as Harrington points out, "clearly concerns the coming of the Son of Man and how one should behave in anticipation of it. Its message is positive action instead of fearful or lazy inaction."

The God-fearing woman of the first reading engaged in positive productive action, whereas the timid servant of the Gospel parable was so afraid of failure he chose not to act at all.

Feast of Christ the King

Fr. Michael Snyder, MM

Tanzania

Ezekiel 34:11–12, 15–17; Psalm 23; First Corinthians 15:20–26, 28; Matthew 25:31–46

I will seek the lost, and I will bring back the strayed, and I will bind up the injured, and I will strengthen the weak, but the fat and the strong I will destroy. I will feed them with justice.

—*Ezekiel 34:16*

I have always enjoyed today's Gospel passage from Matthew. It is such a long and repetitive piece that seems to exaggerate its point to the extreme, and this is precisely why I enjoy it so much!

Jesus says that "all the nations" stand to be judged. And the criterion he uses is how "the least," the most vulnerable, are treated. Jesus, as king, identifies himself with poor and needy people. He wants us to go out among the most vulnerable and feed them, clothe them, do whatever it takes to better the conditions in their lives. The power to choose good and evil is within the reach of all. Jesus wants us to choose goodness. The truly generous are the truly wise. The hand that gives, gathers.

Today we celebrate the feast of Christ the King. The readings emphasize what a king does: he reigns over his people. From the prophet Ezekiel to Paul to Matthew's Gospel, we hear that in God's Reign there will be a separation of the good from the bad. But Ezekiel, like Matthew, emphasizes that God will seek out the persecuted, the troubled, the sick, and will bring them under his protection. Ezekiel writes that God will give them the strength they need until they are saved. Matthew extends this theme by saying that God as Jesus depends on us, his followers, to assist in extending the Reign of God throughout the world.

I am a medical university chaplain in Dar es Salaam, Tanzania. My students are the cream of intelligentsia. They were among the top performers in national exams and thus selected to study here. And they come from all over the country, so there is rich ethnic diversity among them. The university is located adjacent to the national hospital with 1,200 beds.

I walked into one of the main wards at the hospital recently. All the beds were full, yet more patients were lying on the floor right up to the elevator entrance and main door to the building with nothing but a sponge mattress and sheet for comfort. One is overwhelmed upon entering the scene. Maneuvering between the patients, trying not to step on anyone, I approached the patient who had called and asked for my services. As we prayed, others asked if I could spend some time with them. No one cared that I was not African. No one asked for material assistance. They simply wanted prayer and to be strengthened in the faith that says I am not alone in my affliction. God is here with me. I'm a member of God's kingdom and no matter what happens, all will somehow be well.

The medical students can get discouraged when they enter the wards. The challenges seem so great! That's why this Gospel passage is so helpful. It keeps repeating over and over the theme: "Just as you did it to one of the least of these . . . you did to me. . . . Just as you did not do it to one of the least of these, you did not do it to me."

Our hospital is just a microcosm of so many places in the developing world where "the least," the most vulnerable, cry out to their king. And Jesus Christ as king looks to the nations and says I depend upon you to bring relief, healing, peace, and comfort to my people. It is the responsibility of each Christian to assist in the ushering in of God's Reign. And for those who respond generously, giving of themselves freely out of love, God will say: "Come, you that are blessed by my Father, inherit the kingdom prepared for you from the foundation of the world; for I was hungry and you gave me food, I was thirsty and you gave me something to drink, I was a stranger and you welcomed me, I was naked and you gave me clothing, I was sick and you took care of me, I was in prison and you visited me. . . . Truly I tell you, just as did it to one of the least of these . . . , you did to me."

Contributors

Scripture Index